L A B   M A N U A L
T O   A C C O M P A N Y

Pascal's Triangle

Lab Manual to Accompany

Pascal's Triangle

THINK 4.0 Version

Rick Decker & Stuart Hirshfield

HAMILTON COLLEGE

WADSWORTH PUBLISHING COMPANY

Belmont, California

A Division of Wadsworth, Inc.

Computer Science Editor: **Frank Ruggirello**

Editorial Assistant: **Rhonda Gray**

Production Editor: **Donna Linden**

Managing Designer: **Andrew Ogus**

Print Buyer: **Barbara Britton**

Permissions Editor: **Peggy Meehan**

Cover and Text Designer: **Al Burkhardt**

Cover Photographs: **Granite:** © Westlight/H. D. Thoreau

Clouds: © Tony Stone Worldwide/John Chard

Copy Editor: **George Dyke**

Compositor: **Thompson Type, San Diego, California**

Printer: **Malloy Lithographing, Ann Arbor, Michigan**

THINK Pascal is a registered trademark of Symantec Corporation. Macintosh is a trademark of Apple Computer, Inc.

2   3   4   5   6   7   8   9   10—96   95   94   93   92

ISBN 0-534-16177-4

C O N T E N T S

P R E F A C E

We say in the Preface of the accompanying text, *Pascal's Triangle*, that the key pedagogical feature of this package is its reliance on directed laboratory exercises. This manual reflects this orientation. Where the text provides static descriptions of abstract principles (that is, the Pascal language and programming techniques), the lab exercises provide a means for active experimentation that makes the concepts developed in the text tangible and meaningful — real — to students. Indeed, we view the text as a supplement to this manual, as opposed to the other way around.

Organization

Each of the lab sessions (one per chapter of the text) begins with a brief description of the programming and Pascal language concepts to be addressed, a review of the Program in Progress (PIP) that illustrates these concepts, and a listing of specific lab objectives. The exercises that follow typically begin with instructions to run the PIP, since it provides the point of departure for subsequent exercises. (As a result, students spend less time typing and more time programming.) Most of the exercises involve modifying, testing, and expanding the PIP in specific ways that require an understanding of the programming and system-specific concepts involved. Some of the exercises are more exploratory, in that they encourage students to design and perform a test that tells them something about Pascal and to write down the answer in their lab book. Most of the labs contain a "Rehash" section, in which we review topics that are particular to the labs — programming tips and features of the compiler. Finally, "Post-Lab Exercises" are provided at the end of each lab, which may require students to develop the PIP even further or to apply the same principles demonstrated in the PIP to an altogether new problem. We use these Post-Lab Exercises as a source of homework assignments.

In adopting this lab-based approach we make no explicit assumptions about how the course is organized. As we mention in the text, we have run our course in three different ways, depending on how rigid our lab schedules have been. All of the following arrangements have worked well for us:

- Closed, scheduled lab sessions with the instructor and teaching assistants available for help.
- More flexibly scheduled open lab sessions, with a teaching assistant available in the evenings for consultation.
- No scheduled sessions at all, where we rely on the students to complete the labs on their own. Each lab has been carefully developed so that students can work through it on their own, without instructor intervention.

All that matters is that the lab exercises get done while, after, or before (in our order of preference) the corresponding chapter in the text is covered in class. Each set of exercises is designed to take from one to three hours at the machine, depending upon the students' preparation and the amount of experimentation that they choose to conduct. It has been our experience that almost all of the labs require less than the two 75-minute lab periods we allot.

What You'll Need

Before beginning the labs, a quick word is in order about the programming environment on which this manual is based. While a variety of Macintosh hardware configurations work well (such as a hard disk or a hard disk and a floppy drive), we assume that at the very least the students will have access to some model of a Macintosh computer (a Mac Plus, Mac SE, or Mac II) with at least 1 megabyte of internal memory and two 800K floppy disk drives. The manual also is written with the assumption that students are comfortable with standard Macintosh terminology and protocols. That is, they should have a general familiarity with the Macintosh desktop and should know how to use the mouse, menus, windows, and basic keyboard techniques, such as command-key equivalents. If this is not the case, we advise our students to take a Macintosh "Guided Tour" using a disk available from Apple.

As regards the Pascal system, this manual describes the implementation of *Pascal's Triangle* that uses Symantec's THINK Pascal (version 4.0, although one can use version 2.0 or 3.0 as well—there are some minor differences that are explained in the labs). We assume that students have access to Disk 1 of the standard THINK package (an 800K disk containing at least the files *THINK Pascal*, *Runtime.lib*, and *Interface.lib*); a startup disk containing a System Folder that is customized to the machine and printing environment that the class will be working in (containing System version 4.2 and Finder version 6.0, or newer); and a third blank 800K diskette, which can be used for storing copies of programs. The manuals that come with THINK Pascal (which we will abbreviate TP) may at times be useful, but they are not essential to using our package. We will describe those features of TP that we will use in the lab exercises as we need them.

Finally, we should note that there are minor differences between the programs listed in the text and those that have been recorded on the accompanying disk. Generally speaking, the differences are the result of the fact that the text versions of the programs are generic (although not perfectly "standard") Pascal, whereas the disk versions are specific to a particular implementation of Pascal.

The THINK Pascal versions differ from the text listings in the following ways:

1. The *Setup* procedure introduced in Lab 3 and used in all subsequent disk PIPs is Macintosh-specific and is not included in the text PIPs.
2. Programs that make explicit use of Pascal files (the PIPs for Chapters 11 and 12) use THINK-specific versions of the *reset*, *rewrite*, and *close* procedures and do not include file names in the program parameter list.

Pascal's Triangle

Computer Science and Programming: An Introduction to Pascal

L A B O R A T O R Y

Introduction

This set of lab exercises is somewhat different from those that will follow in at least three important ways. First of all, out of necessity it focuses on using the THINK Pascal (TP) system as opposed to the Pascal language per se. We must get through these "system" preliminaries in order for you to begin developing your programming expertise in subsequent chapters. Second, whereas most labs will begin with a Program in Progress (PIP) that is described in the text, in this case you don't yet know enough Pascal to make much sense of the program. Not to worry—we'll guide you through it so that you can make it work and understand its output. Finally, in all other labs you are provided with a copy of the PIP as the starting point for your lab exercises. Given that the primary purpose of this chapter's lab is to show you how to use TP to create working programs, you begin this lab on your own, by typing in and running your first Pascal program.

L A B   O B J E C T I V E S

In this lab, we will:

- Show you how to set up and back up your TP disks.
- Show you how to start the TP system.

- Introduce you to the basic facilities of TP, including those for:
  - Entering, editing, and saving programs.
  - Creating, saving, and running projects.
  - Debugging programs, to find and remove errors.
- Show you how to quit the TP system.

Exercises

1. Building Your Working Disk

The following instructions assume that you have (1) a floppy disk that has been initialized and already contains a System Folder appropriate to your computer (we will refer to this as your *System Disk* from now on); (2) Disk 1 of the THINK Pascal package; (3) the Pascal's Triangle disk that comes with this package; and (4) two new, blank 800K floppy disks. (See your instructor if conditions vary.)

To get started, you need to initialize your blank disks. To do that, proceed as follows:

a. Put your System Disk into the Mac. Disks are always inserted with the metal tab first, arranged so that the notched corner of the disk is to your right. Turn on the Mac using the power switch on the back (if the Mac is a Plus or SE model) or at the top center of the keyboard (on Macintosh II models).

b. Insert one of the blank disks into the remaining slot. (By the way, it doesn't matter which disks go into which slots, as long as the System Disk goes in first.)

c. You'll get a message that the blank disk is unreadable. Don't panic; just tell the machine to *initialize* it by clicking in the box labeled *2-sided*.

d. After some whirring and waiting, you will be asked to name the disk. You will be using this disk to make backups of programs that you are working on and to hand in your assignments. Title it with your name. We will refer to this disk as your *Data Disk*.

e. Eject your Data Disk by dragging it (that is, use the mouse to position the arrow on the disk's icon [its small picture], press and hold the mouse button, and drag the picture) to the Trash Can icon. Don't worry—this will not "trash" your disk. It is simply a direct way of ejecting a single disk.

f. Insert the Pascal's Triangle disk that came with this package into the vacant drive. Double-click the disk icon to open it onto the desktop. As you can now see, the disk contains 12 folders, one for each chapter of the text (except for the first). Drag all 12 items from the Pascal's Triangle disk to your System Disk (you can do this all at once by clicking and dragging so as to "surround" all 12 folders). After the copying is completed, eject the Pascal's Triangle disk.

g. Now, insert the other blank disk and initialize it, as in steps b–d. Name this disk *TP Disk*, as we will use it to create a backup copy of one of the THINK Pascal disks.

h. Eject your System Disk by dragging it into the trash.

i. Insert Disk 1 from the TP package into the vacant drive. Notice the icon appearing on the screen for the "THINK Pascal 1" disk. Double-click on this icon to see a window describing the disk's contents. Drag the three files *THINK Pascal, Interface.lib*, and *Runtime.lib* to the icon representing your TP Disk. (*Note*: You may be asked to temporarily reinsert your System Disk and then replace it with your TP Disk. Just do what the Mac tells you to do.) After the copying is complete, eject the THINK Pascal 1 disk and reinsert your System Disk.

j. In general, this is how you will operate — with your System Disk in one drive and your TP Disk in the other. As you create programs, you will save them on the System Disk. When you want to make a copy of a program (to back it up or to hand in), you will eject the TP Disk, insert the disk with your name on it, and drag the program's icon from the System Disk to your Data Disk.

k. Choose **Restart** from the **Special** menu. If all goes well, you are now ready to use the THINK Pascal (TP) system.

l. Put the original TP disk and the original Pascal's Triangle disk in a safe place. From now on you'll work from your System disk (containing a System Folder and the 12 Pascal's Triangle folders) and the backup TP disk (containing *THINK Pascal, Runtime.lib*, and *Interface.lib*).

2. Introducing THINK Pascal

a. Open THINK Pascal by double-clicking on its icon.

b. A *dialog box* will then appear waiting for you to choose a *project* to open. A project is a translated (object-code) version of a program along with several object-code versions of support files that are required to run your program. TP does not literally run *programs*; rather, it runs *projects* — collections of already-translated programs. It's helpful to keep in mind an automotive metaphor: Think of a project as a car and a program as the driver. By itself, a car can do nothing — it just contains all the systems needed for the driver to do what he or she wants. Similarly, a program without a project to run it is like a driver without a car. You'll see later that we will use the same project to support many different programs: All we'll do is remove the old program and replace it with a new one, just as several drivers might use the same car at different times.

Program   **Project**

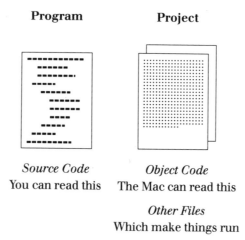

Source Code   *Object Code*

You can read this   The Mac can read this

Other Files

Which make things run

Program + Project = Runnable Application

Click on **New** in the dialog box to signal that you want to create your own project. (Your dialog box may look slightly different from the one illustrated here.)

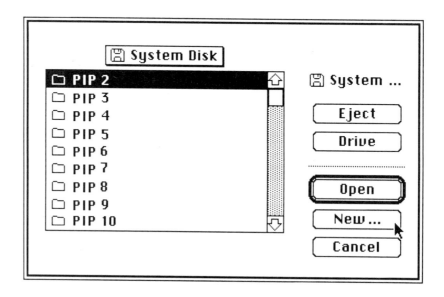

You'll store working versions of your programs and projects on the System Disk. To choose a drive between the two available disks, just click the **Drive** button in the dialog box before you click the **New** button.

c. Another *dialog box* will prompt you to name the project you want to create. Type 'First Project' (without the quotes) and click in the **Create** button.

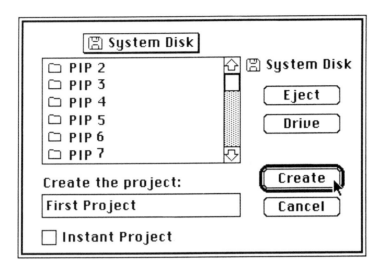

d. A window will appear, titled First Project, containing two support files, *Runtime.lib* and *Interface.lib*. These will be part of every project you create in this course. This window is referred to as the *Project window*. It displays information about the current project, which, in this case, is First Project.

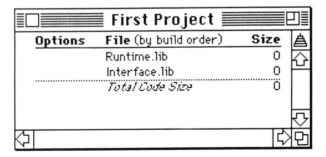

e. First Project includes the requisite support files but, as of yet, contains no main program. We could use the **Open** command from the **File** menu to open an existing program, but you will be typing a new program, so choose the **New** item from the **File** menu instead.

f. A new window will appear. This is referred to as the *Program window*, and it displays a human-readable (text) version of a Pascal program. This window is where you will type and edit programs.

3. Entering a Program

a. Quickly review the Chapter 1 Program in Progress (PIP), named *Zeller*. Then, type the program into the Program window *exactly* as it appears. Don't leave *anything* out (like the semicolons or the period at the end). Be sure to hit the Return key after the period at the end. If any line goes out of the window on the right side, you can make the window larger by using the mouse to drag its *grow box* (in the lower-right corner of the window) to the right.

You'll notice that you don't have to put spaces or tabs at the start of each line. In fact, you don't even have to press the Return key at the end of a line, except for the last line. TP takes care of the "prettyprinting" for you. That is, it does its best to recognize when you have typed in Pascal reserved words, displays them in boldface type, and indents the program to reflect this interpretation. If TP detects an obvious error (like a misspelled reserved word or a missing punctuation mark) that keeps it from being able to translate a particular statement, it will display the statement in outline typeface, beginning at the point in the line where it stopped making sense to TP. Such errors usually involve simple typing mistakes that can be corrected by using the Backspace key and then retyping. Also, note that an **Edit** menu containing the standard Macintosh operations of **Cut**, **Copy**, **Paste**, and **Undo** is available as you work in the Program window.

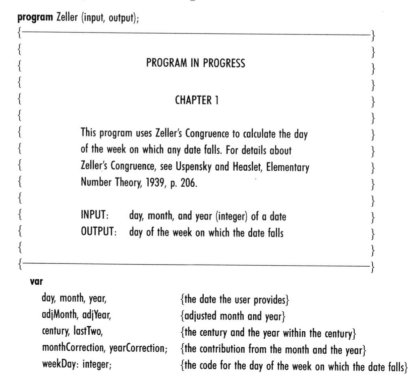

```
program Zeller (input, output);
{―――――――――――――――――――――――――――――――――――――――――――}
{                                                              }
{                      PROGRAM IN PROGRESS                     }
{                                                              }
{                           CHAPTER 1                          }
{                                                              }
{     This program uses Zeller's Congruence to calculate the day   }
{     of the week on which any date falls. For details about   }
{     Zeller's Congruence, see Uspensky and Heaslet, Elementary }
{     Number Theory, 1939, p. 206.                             }
{                                                              }
{     INPUT:     day, month, and year (integer) of a date      }
{     OUTPUT:    day of the week on which the date falls        }
{                                                              }
{―――――――――――――――――――――――――――――――――――――――――――}
    var
        day, month, year,             {the date the user provides}
        adjMonth, adjYear,            {adjusted month and year}
        century, lastTwo,             {the century and the year within the century}
        monthCorrection, yearCorrection;   {the contribution from the month and the year}
        weekDay: integer;             {the code for the day of the week on which the date falls}
```

```
begin
  {————————— GET THE DAY, MONTH, AND YEAR —————————}
  writeln('At the prompt, ">", enter numbers for day, month, year');
  writeln('Separate the numbers by spaces, and press Return after entering all three. ');
  write('>');
  readln(day, month, year);
  {————————— ADJUST THE MONTH AND YEAR —————————}
  {Since February is the only month that has a variable number of days, the program}
  {treats January and February as the last two months of the previous year.        }
  if month <= 2 then
    begin   {We only do this part if the month entered was Jan. or Feb.}
      adjMonth := 10 + month;
      adjYear := year - 1
    end
  else
    begin   {We do this part if the month entered was not Jan. or Feb.}
      adjMonth := month - 2;
      adjYear := year
    end;
  {————————— CALCULATE THE DAY CODE —————————}
  {This is where the real work goes on. "weekDay" gets set to}
  {a whole number in the range 0 .. 6, which is interpreted as}
  {the day Sunday .. Saturday, respectively.                 }
  monthCorrection := (26 * adjMonth - 2) div 10;              {adjustment for
                                                               the month}

  century := adjYear div 100;
  lastTwo := adjYear mod 100;
  yearCorrection := lastTwo + (lastTwo div 4) + (century div 4) + 5 * century;  {adjustment for
                                                               the year}

  weekDay := (day + monthCorrection + yearCorrection) mod 7;
  {————————— CONVERT THE DAY CODE, WRITE THE RESULT —————————}
  writeln;
  write(day : 1, '.', month : 1, '.', year : 1, ' falls on ');
  case weekDay of
    0:
      writeln('Sunday');
    1:
      writeln('Monday');
    2:
      writeln('Tuesday');
    3:
      writeln('Wednesday');
```

```
          4:
             writeln('Thursday');
          5:
             writeln('Friday');
          6:
             writeln('Saturday')
       end
    end.
```

b. Once you complete your typing, save the program by choosing the **Save As...** command from the **File** menu. Another dialog box will appear, and you can save the program by typing in 'First.p' (again, without the quotes) and clicking the **Save** button. Save your program on the System Disk, where it can keep the project company.

4. Checking and Editing a Program

a. You can now ask TP to check your program for syntax errors (errors in the use of the Pascal language that would keep TP from translating your program) by choosing **Check Syntax** from the **Run** menu. Do so now.

b. It just might happen that you will make some sort of error in the future. To prepare you for that, let's try to generate and fix some errors in a controlled situation. Place the "I-beam" cursor after a semicolon at the end of a line in the Program window, by moving it to that position and then clicking the button. Press the Backspace key to erase the semicolon. Check the syntax of your program and see what happens.

c. The *Bug window* will appear, along with an annoying beep. Read the message and then click the mouse button to make it go away. Notice that the clever TP compiler will point to the line in your program where it thinks the error is. Put the semicolon back to restore your program to its pristine state. Use **Check Syntax** until no errors are found to make sure the program is restored.

d. While you are making mistakes, you probably do not want to instruct TP to save any changes in your program. That will keep a virgin copy of your program on disk, safe from harm, while you modify a copy of the program in memory.

e. Try to make and fix some other errors.

    i. Near the top of the program, there is a line containing the word **var**, followed by a line that begins with the word *day*. Drag across *day* and the comma that follows so that *day* and the comma are highlighted. Select **Cut** from the **Edit** menu to eliminate them. (After you've seen what happens, you can restore what you cut by moving the I-beam to where the deleted material should go, clicking there, and choosing **Paste** from the **Edit** menu.)

    ii. Change the spelling of any word in the program.

iii. Delete the period at the end of the program.

iv. Change *adjMonth* := 10 + *month*; to *adjMonth* = 10 + *month*; by eliminating the colon before the equals sign.

f. If you get hopelessly lost in making and fixing errors, ask for help. (This will be the last time you'll be reminded to ask for help.) If, on the other hand, you've managed to enter the program so that it is acceptable syntactically to TP (which you can tell because Checking it produces no error messages), choose **Save** from the **File** menu to save the corrected text version of your program.

5. Projects: Running a Program

a. In order to run a program, we must do more than save it in its text form — we must incorporate it into a project. *Remember*: Users create programs, TP runs projects. You can add your version of the *Zeller* program to your First Project by selecting **Add File...** from the **Project** menu. Another dialog box will appear, asking what file you wish to add to the project. Click once on the word *First.p* and then click on the **Add...** button.

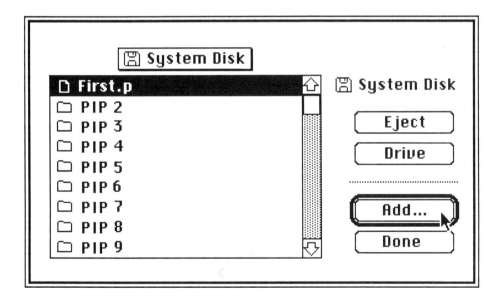

You will notice that **program** *First.p* is now part of the Project window. There is only one user-created file for this program, so when the Add File dialog box appears again, just click the **Done** button.

b. Now you're ready to see what happens when we run First Project.

When First Project runs, another of TP's windows — the *Text window* — will appear on the screen. The Text window is used by TP to communicate with us in text while a project is running. For example, the Text window is where TP displays the textual output (there can be graphical output as well) produced by a project. It is also where we can provide text input to a running project. In this case, it will serve both purposes.

You can take a look at the Text window now, by selecting **Text** from the **Windows** menu. A little bitty window will appear, one that will certainly be too small for our purposes. This is a good time to resize it by dragging the grow box in the lower-right corner of the window. You can also move the Text window (or any of TP's other windows) by positioning the pointer in the *title bar* at the top of the window and dragging it where you wish.

Let's see what *Zeller* does. Pull down the **Run** menu and select the **Go** item.

First, a message requesting input (a *prompt*) is displayed in the Text window, and then TP waits until we provide enough data so that it can continue its processing. **Program** *Zeller* requires that we enter three integers (separated by blanks or returns, followed by a Return) representing the day, month, and year for which we want to know the day of the week.

Try entering today's date. Is it right? If not, did you enter the day first, then the month, and then the *entire* year (or are you asking *Zeller* for a date 1900 years ago)? Use *Zeller* to find the day of the week on which you were born. Call home tonight and check.

There's a good chance that the program won't work the way you expect. Don't panic! First see if you can figure out what happened — it will almost certainly be due to mistyping. Check the listing of *Zeller* as it appears here and see if you can find the error in your version. If you do, drag over the offending part, retype it, and try again. Trying again will involve re-Checking the program's syntax. You can, though, change your program and simply rerun the same project. TP is aware that you have changed the text version of your program and will ask your permission to save it and incorporate the new version into the existing project. If it still keeps blowing up in your face, ask for help — that's what labs are for.

6. Experiments

In this section, we will explore some Pascal language features. There are some blank spaces here, which you might want to fill in for future reference (such as for quizzes).

a. The **begin..end** pair of words are statement *grouping* words. In effect, they act like parentheses to collect statements that are to be considered as a single unit. We will explore this concept in more detail later. For now, what happens if you add several matched **begin**s and **end**s to your program? What happens if you add a **begin** that's not matched with a subsequent **end**?

b. Semicolons in Pascal are statement *separators*, in that they tell the compiler that one statement has ended and another is about to begin.

    i. With this in mind, can you explain why there is no semicolon at the end of a line just before an **end**?

    ii. Try putting in several semicolons in place of one. Your program should still run just fine (unless your semicolons were placed inside the **case** statement). Why? Does it help to know that there are such things as *empty statements*, which are invisible in the program listing and do nothing?

c. There is a computer-specific limit to the size of integers. Try running your program to discover what day January 1, 40000 will be. What happens? Why? Ask your instructor.

Try various inputs to see if you can nail down exactly how large an integer can be in THINK Pascal and still be correctly represented.

d. Add the line *writeln*('day mod 7: ', *day* **mod** 7); after the *readln* statement. Then, see if you can figure what the Pascal operator **mod** does, by trying several runs supplying different input values for *day*.

7. Printing

Many times you will need to obtain a printed copy of a program, either because your instructor wants you to hand in a copy of your program or because you would like to study the program at your leisure. You can do this by making the Program window active (by clicking in it) and then selecting **Print...** from the **File** menu. The exact details of how to print vary from one installation to another, so ask your instructor how to print in your local environment, and then make a printed copy of *Zeller* so you can see how it's done. Below, for your own reference, make note of the steps you need to print a program.

8. Quitting

a. Save the final version of your program by using **Save** from the **File** menu.

b. Choose **Quit** from the **File** menu. This will get you out of the TP application and back to the Mac desktop.

c. Select **Shut Down** from the **Special** menu. The disks will pop out. Take them with you.

d. Turn off the Mac.

e. Leave.

Rehash

- It is always a good idea to work on a *copy* of a program such as TP. That way, if you lose a disk or one gets inadvertently damaged, you're not out the money you spent for TP or *Pascal's Triangle*.

- Store your original disks safely. Safe storage of disks includes the obvious, like not using them for coffee mug coasters or dropping them in the mud. In addition, since data are stored magnetically on disks, you should not put them near strong magnets (like those in telephones or stereo speakers). Other than these cautions, disks are fairly robust: You can carry them in a pocket without fear (but don't sit on them).

- TP is a complete programming environment, which includes facilities for entering, editing, saving, translating, running, debugging, and organizing Pascal programs. The first four of these tasks are accomplished on text versions of a program. The remaining tasks involve a *project*—that is, a source version of your program plus additional files that the computer needs in order to run your program. In order to run a program, it must first be translated successfully and then incorporated into a project.

Post-Lab Exercises

1. The best — and only *real* — way to get familiar with the TP system is to use it. For typing and program-editing practice, try entering and compiling any of the Programs in Progress from later chapters in the text.

2. A nice aspect of modern programming environments like TP is that they're easy enough to use that if there's a language feature you'd like to explore, all you have to do is write a little program to try it out. Usually, all your program will have to do is *readln* some information, use that in a statement or two that you want to try, and *writeln* some results. You might want to try some of the samples we've listed below, along with some of your own. Curiosity and a venturesome attitude are good things. Don't worry about breaking things — it's hard to do serious damage in the world of cyberspace.

```
program Tester (input, output);
    var
        myInteger, i : integer;    {Use any names you want here, but make sure to name anything you
                                    use.}
begin
    write('Type in something: ');
    readln(myInteger);

    {You'll change this part to try new features.}
    { ------------------------------------------------------------------------------------- }
    if myInteger > 100 then
        writeln('Big number')
    else
        writeln('Small number')
    { ------------------------------------------------------------------------------------- }
end.
```

You might try replacing the part of this program within bracketed lines with one of the following. See if you can guess what the statements will do.

```
a. writeln(myInteger div 4)
b. write('DOG');
   writeln('FOOD');
   writeln('CAT');
   writeln('NIP')
c. writeln('Well');
   writeln;
   writeln('Well, well!')
d. for i := 1 to 5 do
       writeln('Repetition ', i)
e. for i := 1 to myInteger do
       write('Repetition ', i)
```

CHAPTER

2 Problem Solving and Programs: Primitive Data Types and Statements

L A B O R A T O R Y

Introduction

From this point on in our lab sessions our emphasis will shift from using TP to understanding and using the Pascal language. While we will continue to develop our facility with TP as a programming tool, we will concentrate on the programming language and process. In this and all subsequent labs the Program in Progress will serve as our starting and ending points. It provides us with both a vehicle for Pascal experimentation and a source of programming "building blocks," which we will copy for use in other programs.

The Chapter 2 PIP, as described in the text, acts like an automated tax preparation tool. It makes use of Pascal's primitive data types and statements—the assignment, *readln*, and *writeln* statements. We'll use it to understand these basic ingredients of all Pascal programs.

L A B   O B J E C T I V E S

In this lab, we will:

- Help you to use and understand the Chapter 2 PIP, *TaxMan*.
- Guide you in experimenting with declarations involving some of Pascal's primitive data types: *integer*, *real*, and *char*.
- Guide you in experimenting with the assignment, *readln*, and *writeln* statements.
- Illustrate Pascal's rules for type coercion, which describe how expressions involving more than one data type get evaluated.

- Show you how to use some of TP's debugging facilities — the Observe and Instant windows, and the Stepping command.
- Have you expand the PIP to perform and report additional calculations.

Exercises

1. Reusing a Project

For this and all subsequent chapters, we have already prepared the Program in Progress, so you don't have to type it in. If you followed the instructions from the Chapter 1 lab exercises properly, 12 files or folders (one per chapter, excluding Chapter 1) containing the PIPs now reside on your System Disk.

Turn on your computer and click on your program icon, *First.p*. Then select **Get Info** from the **File** menu (or choose the command equivalent by holding the command key, ⌘, while pressing the 'I' key). You'll see that *First.p* takes about 5K bytes on the disk (a K in computer terminology is 1024 bytes, and a byte is big enough to store a character). Now find the size of First Project. Wow! 105K bytes. There are only 800K total bytes available on the disk, so we clearly don't have room to make a new project for each program. What we'll do is reuse an old project. Rename First Project by clicking on its icon and typing the new name, *Generic.π* (you can type 'π' by holding the Option key down while you type 'p'). In the labs, we'll use the convention that projects will have names ending in '.π' and programs will have names ending in '.p'.

We'll now change *Generic.π* to run the Lab 2 PIP.

a. Double-click on *Generic.π* to start TP and open the project.

b. Select the program *First.p* by clicking on its name in the *Generic.π* Project window and choose **Remove** from the **Project** menu. This will remove the compiled code from your project and sever the link between the program and the project. Don't worry — the Pascal source code still resides in the program *First.p*. Recall our car and driver metaphor from Lab 1 — we're about to replace drivers (*First.p* goes out, and *TaxMan.p* goes in) in the same car (the project).

c. Go to the **Project** menu again and select **Add File...**. You'll see a dialog box asking what file to add to the project, just as you did in Lab 1. Find the PIP 2 folder, double-click it, then select *TaxMan.p* and click the **Add...** button, and the Lab 2 PIP will be added to your project. When the dialog box comes up again, click the **Done** button, indicating that there are no more files to add to the project.

We'll perform the same sequence of steps in most of the rest of the labs, modifying Generic.π to run each lab's programs. *Note:* You'll have to remove the old program each time, since a project may contain only one program at a time.

2. Backing Up Programs

We will be editing the *TaxMan* program during the course of these exercises, so let's save a copy of the original in case we need to refer to it later.

a. Bring up the *TaxMan.p* Program window by double-clicking on the *TaxMan.p* line in the Project window.

b. The Program window is now the active window. (Notice that only one TP window is active at any one time. Many operations, like the one we are about to invoke, apply to the active window—so be careful. The window whose title bar is shaded is the active window.)

c. Select **Save As...** from the **File** menu. The **Save As...** command lets us save the current file under another name, which you provide in the dialog box that appears.

d. Title the file *My TaxMan.p*. Subsequent editing will then apply to this new copy of the file but not to the original.

e. If the dialog box has a header that says "System Disk," the backup will be saved on the System Disk, which is where we want it. If the header says "TP Disk," click on the **Drive** button to change where saving will be done.

f. Save the copy by clicking the **Save** button in the dialog box. Notice that TP is smart enough to recognize that you have renamed a program file and adjusts the TaxMan project accordingly.

3. Watching Your Program Run

Now run the program, by selecting **Go** from the **Run** menu. When you are first asked for an input value, wait.

Notice the can of "bug spray" in the upper-right corner of the screen. Click on it now. Doing so interrupts the execution of the project and returns control to you. It might take a few clicks to synchronize the interruption. You can now use any of TP's editing and/or debugging facilities. We'll do both.

a. First, click on the Bug window to remove it, then move and resize the Text window to cover the middle of the screen. We need it larger so that all of the program's prompts will fit nicely in the window. Recall that you size a window by dragging its grow box in the lower-right corner of the window.

b. Next, move and resize the Program window so that it covers the top third of the screen and doesn't overlap the Text window.

c. Now choose **Observe** from the **Debug** menu (or the **Windows** menu, if you're using TP 2.0). Another of TP's windows, the (surprise!) *Observe window*, appears. Move this one to the bottom of the screen. By typing in the names of variables or constants from our program, we can *observe* their values as the current project runs. Type in the names *STANDARDDEDUC-TION*, *single*, *numberDependents*, and *campaignFund* (each followed by a Return) in the Observe window.

```
┌─────────────────────────────────────────────────────┐
│ ▤□▦▦▦▦▦▦▦▦▦▦ Observe ▦▦▦▦▦▦▦▦▦▦ ▣▤ │
├────────────────────┬──────────────────────────────┬──┤
│                    │ STANDARDDEDUCTION            │⇧ │
│                    ├──────────────────────────────┤  │
│                    │ single                       │  │
│                    ├──────────────────────────────┤  │
│                    │ numberDependents             │  │
│                    ├──────────────────────────────┤  │
│                    │ campaignFund                 │  │
│   Enter an expression │                            │  │
│                    │                              │  │
│                    │                              │⇩ │
├─┬──┬───────────────┴──────────────────────────────┼──┤
│⇦│  │▨▨▨▨▨▨▨▨▨▨▨▨▨▨▨▨▨▨▨▨▨▨▨▨▨▨▨▨▨▨▨▨│⇨▣│
└─┴──┴────────────────────────────────────────────────┴──┘
```

d. We could continue program execution from the *readln* statement where we stopped by selecting **Go** from the **Run** menu, but we'll use another TP command instead.

Notice where the pointing finger is in your program window. It should be at the statement *readln(single)*, indicating that this statement is the one about to be executed. Select **Step Over** from the **Run** menu to resume execution, or use its command-key equivalent, ⌘-J. (If you're using an older version of TP, select **Step** from the **Run** menu, or use ⌘-S.) This command executes your program one line at a time, so you can watch what happens at a leisurely pace. You'll have to enter 's' (without the quotes) from the keyboard, since the *readln* statement is expecting some character input.

Step through the program, using ⌘-J repeatedly and entering values when needed. Keep an eye on the Observe window and watch the values for the quantities we entered. When a project is misbehaving—that is, it is running, but not in the way we expected or hoped it would—you can use the Observe window to monitor the values of important quantities as they vary during execution.

e. We can even change the values of variables during breaks in execution by means of TP's *Instant window*. Select **Instant** from the **Debug** menu now. Make sure the Observe window is visible, then type the statement *single* : = 'n'; into the Instant window, and click the **Do It** button. Notice in the Observe window how the value of variable *single* has changed.

Change the value of variable *numberDependents* to 2 by typing *numberDependents* : = 2; into the Instant window and clicking **Do It**.

Try using the Instant window to change the value of variable *single* to 2, by typing *single* : = 2; into the Instant window. The message that appears is telling you that 2 is not a permissible value for a variable of **type** *char*, like *single*. This is an example of a *run-time error*—one that cannot necessarily be detected while TP is translating a program, but rather comes up during the course of executing a project.

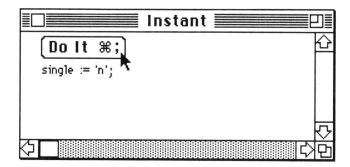

The Instant window is useful for trying out new code or fixes to existing code while a project is running. It also provides a quick and realistic means for experimentation.

f. Now run the program to completion.

4. Notes on Program Style

Let's take a minute to review our PIP in terms of programming style. While the notion of a program having style may seem far-fetched to you, remember that programs are not written just for computers. People have to read, maintain, and update them. Indeed, much of a professional programmer's time is spent reviewing and revising existing programs. Just because a program runs does not mean that it is a good program. Here are some things to consider.

a. Variable names. Do the names of the variables reflect the quantities they represent? A variable called *taxableIncome* tells the reader a lot more about what it represents than does one named *t*.

b. Constants. There is one quantity, *STANDARDDEDUCTION*, in this program that always remains the same. It is generally better to single such terms out as constants at the head of the program. For instance,

const
    STANDARDDEDUCTION = 5100.00;

tells you much more than the naked 5100.00 in the body of the program. Constants are declared just below the program header and before the variable declarations. Notice, there is no colon before the equals sign.

c. Spaces. It is a good idea to separate logically distinct collections of statements by introducing blank lines (just hit the Return key a few times).

d. Comments. Anything within a pair of {*curly braces*} will be ignored by the Pascal translator. A program generally begins with a collection of comments describing what it does. Comments are also useful to annotate any line whose function would not be immediately obvious to a reader.

e. User interface. A good program should be clear to the user as well as to a reader. That's why we included a prompt at each point where the program requires input, so that the operator would know that she or he was expected to type something in at that point. The *write* statement before each *readln* prints a message to the operator—anything within single quotes appears exactly as written. The *writeln* statements that display the results of calculations also include explanations of what is being printed, by including *literals* between single quotes. Also note the *writeln* statement at the end of the program, which indicates clearly for the user that the program has completed its processing.

5. Experiments

Let's try some experiments to see how Pascal works.

a. Can you change the value of a constant within a program by an assignment statement? In other words, if you have declared *STANDARDDEDUCTION* to be the constant 5100.00, could you later make the statement

STANDARDDEDUCTION := 6000.00

Why do you think Pascal was designed this way?

b. Does Pascal allow *type coercion*? For example, if *taxLiability* is a real variable and *numberDependents* is an integer, can you make the assignment *taxLiability* := *numberDependents* or *numberDependents* := *taxLiability*? Try both statements in the Instant window while your program is running. Explain your findings.

c. On the subject of type coercion, Pascal expects a real number to begin with a digit or + or − sign, and to have a decimal point somewhere, followed by one or more digits. If *wagesSalariesTips* is a real variable, can you legally enter 56 as the input to *readln(wagesSalariesTips)*? In reverse, can you enter a real number as input to a *readln* that expects an integer? Try it, entering 0.9 for the number of dependents, and then explain.

d. Notice how the *writeln* statements that display the values of variables do so using *formatted output*. What happens if the format is either too large or too small for the value to print in?

6. Programming on Your Own

Change your version of the *TaxMan* program to accomplish the following. Make the proposed changes incrementally — don't do them all at once! Make a few related changes, Check to be sure you haven't made any syntax errors, and try them out. Use the Observe and Instant windows as necessary to figure how and if your changes are working. Check (by hand, if necessary) that the results are correct.

a. The program calculates *taxLiability* based on a fixed value of 25%. Represent that quantity as a Pascal constant and change the statement that performs the calculation accordingly.

b. Instead of using a constant value for *STANDARDDEDUCTION*, base the calculation of *taxableIncome* on the number of exemptions declared by the user. To accomplish this you will want to:

  i. Eliminate the constant *STANDARDDEDUCTION*.

  ii. Create a new integer variable to represent the number of exemptions for a particular user.

  iii. Prompt the user to enter a value for the number of exemptions.

  iv. Revise the calculation of *taxableIncome* to allow a deduction of $2000 for each exemption claimed.

  v. Change whatever input statements should be changed to reflect this new method of calculation.

Rehash

- The "bug spray" icon in the upper-right corner of TP's screen allows you to interrupt the execution of a program at any time it is running. After you have stopped a program, you may resume execution at the location where you stopped by choosing **Go** or one of the **Step** commands from the **Run** menu.

- If a program is halted during execution, you may begin execution from the start by selecting **Reset** and then **Go** from the **Run** menu. **Reset** clears all current variables and starts the program from the first statement.

- The Observe window allows you to inspect the current value of any constant, variable, or expression. You may cause the Observe window to appear by selecting the **Observe** item from the **Debug** menu.

- The Instant window allows you to execute a Pascal statement, such as an assignment statement, just as if the statement were part of a program. The Instant window is made visible by choosing **Instant** from the **Debug** menu.

- To execute a program one statement at a time, use the **Step Over** command from the **Run** menu. The command key equivalent, ⌘-J, accomplishes the same thing (and reduces the need for excessive mousing around). Stepwise execution is often used in combination with the Observe window to trace the execution of a program.

- When a program is halted (either by the bug spray or between invocations of **Step Over**), the finger icon in the Program window points to the statement that will be executed next.

Post-Lab Exercises

1. Extend the PIP to make its tax calculations more detailed, as follows:
   a. Create and display a new value, *totalIncome*, which is the sum of *wagesSalariesTips* and *interest*.
   b. Solicit a value for *unemploymentCompensation* and include it in the *totalIncome*.
   c. Allow the user to enter two IRA deductions (one for the filer and one for the filer's spouse), which are added together to form a value named *adjustments*.
   d. Recalculate and display *adjGrossIncome* as *totalIncome* − *adjustments*.

2. Write a program from scratch. In particular, write and test (it should go without saying) a program that will do what is asked in Exercise 38 of Chapter 2 of your text.

3 Program Design and Subprograms: Procedures and Functions

L A B O R A T O R Y

Introduction

Subprograms afford us two significant advantages. First, we can speed the programming task by using a collection of already written procedures and functions available to apply to new programming tasks. Such predefined routines may be built in as part of the Pascal language or may be defined by the programmer. Second, subprograms can be used as an organizational tool for programs that are too complicated for us to grasp at first glance. By decomposing a program—redefining it as a collection of smaller, simpler subprograms—we can "hide" or localize the details of calculations and control explicitly the flow of information throughout the program.

Both of these advantages apply to our PIP for this chapter, a program that performs some simple geometrical calculations. After using it to illustrate the mechanics of defining and invoking subprograms, you will extend it to include subprograms of your own devising.

L AB O B J E C T I V E S

In this lab, we will:

- Help you to use and understand the Chapter 3 PIP, *SnowPerson*.
- Guide you in experimenting with Pascal's predefined functions, value and **var** parameters, and local and global variables.

• Illustrate the principles of top-down design in defining procedures and functions that extend the PIP.

Exercises

1. Chapter 3 PIP: *SnowPerson*

The PIP for Chapter 3 calculates the volume of a snowperson consisting of three spheres of snow. The program solicits input values for the radii of the three snowballs and then calculates and displays their total volume.

As you did in Lab 2, change your generic project to include the Lab 3 program now and run it. When you are prompted for the first input value, interrupt the program by clicking the "bug spray" can.

Choose **Text** from the **Windows** menu to display the Text window, size it as needed, and then resume processing by selecting **Go** from the **Run** menu (remember, if you don't want to keep going to the menu, you can use the ⌘-G command-key equivalent). Run the project a few times with differing input values. Notice that all three inputs are real values, but we can enter integers if we wish. We saw in Lab 2 that a *readln* that expects a real input will also accept an integer input and then coerce the value to be real. Verify by hand (or, at least, convince yourself) that the program is working correctly.

2. A New Procedure: *Setup*

In running the programs so far, you have had to display and size the Text window manually. A generally useful subprogram would be one that makes sure that the Text window is displayed and sized appropriately. Such a procedure, named *Setup*, is defined below. It makes use of three predefined TP procedures to establish the size of and display the Text window. The descriptions of the statements are italicized; don't type these descriptions in. Enter your new procedure into the declaration section of your program, after the variable declarations and before the declaration of the **procedure** *Introduction*.

procedure Setup;
{Sets size of text window and brings it to the front.}
{NOTE: Not standard Pascal. This is Mac-specific. }
{Called by : Main   }
   var
     r : Rect;   Rect *is a Mac type that describes a rectangle by the coordinates of its left, top, right, and bottom sides. On the Mac Plus and SE, the screen coordinates range from 0 to 511 horizontally (left to right) and from 0 to 341 vertically (top to bottom).*
begin
   SetRect(r, 10, 155, 510, 250);   *Set the coordinates of the rectangle* r.
   SetTextRect(r);   *Make the Text window the size of* r.
   ShowText   *Show the Text window in its new size.*
end;

Once you've declared *Setup*, have the main program call it first. A procedure is invoked by using its name, so your main program statement part will now look like this:

```
begin   {Main}
  Setup;
  Introduction;
      ⋮
```

Run your project as revised to see what *Setup* does. Pretty neat, eh? Save the revised version of your program.

3. Parameters

Procedure *Setup* is an example of a subprogram that does not require any information from the main program. That is, every time we invoke it, it will perform exactly the same series of operations. Other subprograms, like *ComputeVolume* and *GetRadii*, perform the same basic operations each time they are invoked, but do so on different data items. Each requires that we provide it with some information (in the form of a list of variable names) for it to operate on. When the main program asks *ComputeVolume* to perform a calculation, it provides the procedure with the three radius values (the user's input) it needs to accomplish the calculation. These values are called *parameters*.

ComputeVolume does not change the values of its first three parameters. It simply uses the values to do its processing. Parameters *top*, *middle*, and *bottom* in *ComputeVolume* are known as *value* parameters. The last parameter, *totalVolume*, though, is changed within the procedure; and we need to get the new value back to the main program, which acts as the manager that passes information among its subprograms. That's why *totalVolume* is preceded in the procedure heading with the word **var**. It indicates that *totalVolume* in **procedure** *ComputeVolume* is a *variable* parameter. Its value may be modified within the procedure, and the changes will be reflected back in the main program.

Run the following experiments to see how parameters work. You will use TP's Observe window to watch variables change as the project runs, and you can use TP's **Step** commands to control the pace at which the code is executed so that you can actually see the changes.

a. First, open the Observe window and enter the names *topRadius*, *middleRadius*, *bottomRadius*, *top*, *middle*, and *bottom* into successive cells in the window.

b. Begin execution of the project by choosing **Step Into** from the **Run** menu. **Step Into** causes one statement at a time to be executed, just as does **Step Over**. The difference is that **Step Into** continues the stepping process within any subprograms that are called. Step until the main program is about to invoke *GetRadii*. What are the values of *topRadius* and *middleRadius*?

Step until the program has entered **procedure** *GetRadii*. What are the values of *top* and *middle*?

Step (and provide data) until the final *writeln* of **procedure** *GetRadii*. What are the values of *topRadius*, *middleRadius*, *bottomRadius*, *top*, *middle*, and *bottom*?

Step until control returns to the main program (and *ComputeVolume* is about to be invoked). What are the values of the six variables now?

Continue stepping until **procedure** *ComputeVolume* is completed. Notice particularly how control passes to and from the auxiliary **function** *Sphere-Vol*. Have the values of *top* and *middle* changed as a result of *Compute-Volume*'s being invoked?

    c. Edit the *SnowPerson* program by removing the word **var** from the heading of *GetRadii*. Rerun the above experiments and watch the Observe window to see the difference between variable and value parameters. Reedit your program to include the **var** in *GetRadii*'s heading before continuing.

4. A New Procedure: *DisplayResults*

    Consistent with our interest in modularity and in hiding the details of processing from the main program, let's construct an output procedure analogous to our *GetRadii* procedure. We'll call this *DisplayResults*.

    a. Initially, declare *DisplayResults* as follows, placing it at the end of the subprogram declarations:

```
procedure DisplayResults;
begin
   writeln;
   writeln('The total volume of the snowperson is ', totalVolume : 7 : 2)
end;
```

The two *writeln* statements in the body of the procedure are identical to those that were previously in the main program. Indeed, you can cut and paste to complete the body of the procedure.

b. Now, replace the original *writeln*s in the main program with a call to *DisplayResults*. Check your revised program and run the resulting project. It should work just as the original did. Does it?

c. The good news is that your new procedure works. Furthermore, the main program is ever so slightly more readable and uniform. It invokes five subprograms in order—one to set the Text window, another to provide a description to the user, the third to do input, the fourth to do the required processing, and the last to perform output. The bad news is that you have (because we told you to!) violated one of the guiding principles of program design. As it is now, **procedure** *DisplayResults* uses a *global variable* (*totalVolume*) in accomplishing its task. It is not at all clear in looking at the procedure's heading that this is the case. Allowing subprograms to have access to nonlocal variables (those declared in other parts of the program) is dangerous because it complicates the already difficult task of debugging errors that involve these variables. If this program were to misbehave somehow, and the errors produced seemed to involve the variable *totalVolume*, it wouldn't be obvious to us that **procedure** *DisplayResults* was a candidate in investigating the cause of the error. In a small program like *SnowPerson*, this seems like a modest, almost silly concern; but in a larger program involving tens, hundreds, or even thousands of subprograms, making explicit which subprograms have access to which global variables is an important measure of program clarity and style.

To change *DisplayResults* to use a parameter, you must decide

i. What to name the parameter (names need not be the same as the globals, although you can use global names for parameters, if you wish).

ii. What the Pascal type for the parameter is (it must match the type of the corresponding global).

iii. Whether the parameter should be a variable or value parameter. (What do you think? Does *DisplayResults* need or want to change the value of *totalVolume*?)

Go ahead, now. Rewrite *DisplayResults* to use a parameter, and don't forget to change the main program to call *DisplayResults* properly. Step through the execution of the revised project to make sure that the new parameter gets transmitted properly to your new procedure.

5. Another New Subprogram: *ComputeArea*

As one final exercise, let's take on the task of devising a whole new subprogram. We now want **program** *SnowPerson* to report the surface area of the snowperson (as a real number) as well as its volume. This isn't too difficult, given that we can look up the formula for the surface area of a sphere of radius r. The area is $4\pi r^2$. Answering the following questions will help you to write an appropriate subprogram to accomplish this calculation.

a. In terms of the radius, what is the Pascal version of the formula for the surface area of a sphere?

b. What will you name the new subprogram that performs this calculation?

c. Should your new subprogram be a procedure or a function?

d. How many parameters are needed? Of what type? In what order?

e. Where should the new subprogram be called? Will it require a new subprogram to call it, or will it be called from the main program?

Go ahead, now, and write your new subprogram. It will be easier if you've answered the above questions carefully. Compile your latest version of the program and step through it to make sure it works as you expect (for the inputs 1.0, 2.0, and 3.0 for the three radii, the area should be about 175.93).

Rehash

- We can set the Text window on the Macintosh by using three Mac-specific procedures, as follows:

```
procedure Setup;
{Sets size of text window and brings it to the front.}
{NOTE: Not standard Pascal. This is Mac-specific.  }
{Called by : Main                                  }
    var
        r : Rect;
```

begin
    SetRect(r, 10, 155, 510, 250);
    SetTextRect(r);
    ShowText
end;

- The TP **Step Into** command (keyboard equivalent ⌘-I) steps through a program, entering into the code for each subprogram as it is called. The **Step Over** command skips the code within subprograms.
- Basic questions to ask in defining a subprogram include:
  - What should it be named?
  - Should it be a procedure or a function?
  - How many parameters should it use?
  - What is the type of each parameter?
  - How should the subprogram be invoked?
  - Where should it be called from?
  - What if any changes must be made to the calling program to accommodate the subprogram?

Post-Lab Exercises

1. Revise *SnowPerson* so that it produces approximate (integer) and more precise (real) values for both the snowperson's volume and surface area. That is, it should display two estimates and two more precise values with each run.

2. Revise *SnowPerson* so that it solicits the *diameters* of the snowballs, as opposed to the radii.

3. Return to the *TaxMan* PIP from Chapter 2 and revise it to make use of subprograms. Procedures could be defined for each section of the tax form (such as certification, report income, and so on), and functions could be used to accomplish specific calculations.

4. Rewrite *SnowPerson* so that it doesn't use subprograms. Write an essay comparing the versions with and without subprograms. Which would have been easier to write from scratch? Which is easier to read? Is there some lower limit of complexity, below which using subprograms is more trouble than it's worth?

To Do, or Not to Do

Introduction

The PIP for this chapter is a simple *expert system* — a program designed to mimic the decision-making process of an expert in a particular problem domain (weather prediction, in this case). In this lab we will experiment with some of Pascal's decision-making statements, which allow it to alter its actions dynamically, based upon values that are determined at run-time. These statements allow us to write programs that are more sophisticated from a logical point of view. Our programs are no longer constrained to be strictly sequential in nature. We can now also include *branches*, which prescribe one processing path for data meeting certain conditions and another processing path for data meeting other conditions.

This also means, unfortunately, that analyzing the behavior of a program is potentially more difficult, since we don't know ahead of time exactly which statements in a program will be executed during the course of a particular run. Accordingly, this lab begins with some of TP's additional program-control and debugging facilities and, then, helps you to experiment with and make use of Pascal's **if**, **if..else**, and **case** statements.

L A B   O B J E C T I V E S

In this lab, we will:

- Help you to use TP's Stop Signs to control program execution and to debug programs.
- Help you to apply TP's debugging facilities to the task of running and understanding the Chapter 4 PIP, *Weather*.

- Guide you in experimenting with boolean expressions in Pascal.
- Demonstrate the use and workings of Pascal's **if**, **if..else**, and **case** statements.
- Help you to develop procedures that can be used to check input data before they are processed.
- Describe how you can extend the PIP to consider additional factors in making its decisions.

Exercises

1. Stepping in Style: TP's Stop Signs

You saw in the previous lab how TP allows you to control the execution of a project by stepping through the code. This degree of control is particularly useful either when the program being analyzed is sufficiently small that it is not too tedious to step through, or when there is a particular part of a program that you would like to observe in detail. Up to now, though, stepping has been an all-or-nothing proposition. We have had no way to execute a project normally until a specific section of a program is reached and, then, to interrupt processing and step through that section manually. TP's Stop Signs give us this greater degree of control.

a. Change your generic project to run the Lab 4 program. Click the Program window to make it active if it isn't already active and then select **Stops In** from the **Debug** menu. Notice now that the **Stops In** menu item is checked, which indicates that this option is turned on, and also notice that the left edge of the Program window has gained a vertical margin line.

b. Now move the mouse until the cursor is along the left edge of the Program window and watch what happens. The cursor turns into a stop sign and will remain that way as long as the cursor is at the left edge of the window. You can move the stop sign up and down along the left edge to line it up with any instruction in the Program window (click the window's scroll bar on the right until the line of code you are interested in is visible). Clicking the mouse while the cursor is a stop sign places a stop sign (there can be as many as you want in a program) in front of the Pascal instruction it lines up with. Then, when you choose **Go** from the **Run** menu, your project will execute normally until it reaches an instruction with a stop sign. At that point (*before* executing the instruction) processing is interrupted, and you regain control.

You can now step through the program one instruction at a time, open the Observe window to check the values of important variables, use the Instant window to see how an instruction would affect subsequent processing, or simply select **Go** to resume execution (until the next stop sign is encountered).

```
┌─────────────────────────────────────────────────────────────┐
│ ▤□ ▦▦▦▦▦▦▦▦▦▦▦▦▦▦▦▦▦▦▦▦▦▦▦▦▦▦▦▦▦   Weather.p ▤ │
├─────────────────────────────────────────────────────────────┤
│      writeln                                                  │
│    end;                                                       │
│                                                               │
│    procedure AskQuestions (var feelsLikeRain, isRaining, barFalling, │
│      {ask questions and solicit responses from the user that allow } │
│      {all of the boolean parameters to be set}                │
│      var                                                      │
│        response : char;     {user's response from the keyboard} │
│    begin                                                      │
│                                                               │
│ ▣    write('Does it feel like rain? (enter y for yes; n for no):'); │
│      readln(response);                                        │
│      writeln;                                                 │
│      feelsLikeRain := (response = 'y');                       │
│                                                               │
│ ▣    write('Is it raining now? (enter y for yes; n for no):'); │
│      readln(response);                                        │
│      writeln;                                                 │
│      isRaining := (response = 'y');                           │
│                                                               │
│ ▣◁ □ ▦▦▦▦▦▦▦▦▦▦▦▦▦▦▦▦▦▦▦▦▦▦▦▦▦▦▦▦▦▦▦▦▦▦ │
└─────────────────────────────────────────────────────────────┘
```

Individual stop signs can be removed by selecting them (clicking and holding the mouse button down) and dragging them off the left margin of the Program window. Alternatively, all stop signs can be removed at once by choosing **Pull Stops** from the **Debug** menu.

Practice placing and removing stop signs in the *Weather* Program window.

2. Predicting the Behavior of *Weather*

a. We can use all of TP's debugging facilities to see exactly how the *Weather* program makes its predictions. Make sure the **Stops In** menu item is checked and place stop signs at each *write* statement in **procedure** *Ask-Questions*. Now, open the Observe window and make an entry for the variable *response* and then one for each of the seven boolean variables in the parameter list of *AskQuestions*.

b. Now, choose **Go** from the **Run** menu and wait until TP stops at the first stop sign. At this point, of course, none of the variables in the Observe window have meaningful values. Choose **Go** again and watch what happens after you provide input.

Record what character you entered as a *response* to the first question and the value that was then defined by the program for *feelsLikeRain*.

Choose **Go** to move from one stop sign to the next, recording your input for variable *response* and the value defined for the corresponding boolean variable.

response: *isRaining:*
response: *rainPredicted:*
response: *bunionsAche:*
response: *barRising:*
                    barSteady:
                    barFalling:

Choose **Go** one final time and see what prediction the program makes. Rerun the project a few times with different sets of responses. See if you can find two different sets of responses that produce the same prediction.

3. Boolean Expressions

Program *Weather* uses simple boolean expressions to assign values to the variables listed above. To understand how *Weather* actually uses these variables to make its predictions, we will need to analyze **function** *DetermineScore* and **procedure** *MakePrediction*.

a. Select **Pull Stops** from the **Debug** menu to remove all current stop signs from **program** *Weather*. Then place stop signs as follows: (1) before each **if** statement of **function** *DetermineScore*, and (2) before each *writeln* statement in **procedure** *MakePrediction*. Also, add variable *score* to those in the Observe window.

b. Rerun the project with one of the sets of inputs that you recorded before. Watch carefully as the value of *score* gets calculated in *DetermineScore*. Each **if** statement gets executed in order. Its boolean expression is evaluated, and, if the expression is *true*, *score* is updated accordingly. For the first two **if** statements you should be able to predict their actions by looking at the values of the corresponding variables in the Observe window. Select **Go** until you reach the stop sign at the **if** (*isRaining* **and** *barSteady*) **then** . . . statement.

c. You can, in fact, enter any expression directly into the Observe window (variables, after all, are just examples of simple expressions). Enter *isRaining* **and** *barSteady* into the Observe window. Do the same for *rainPredicted* **and** *barFalling* as well as **not**(*isRaining* **or** *feelsLikeRain*) **and** *barRising*.

d. Continue running the project until you reach the stop sign in **procedure** *MakePrediction*. Look at the value of variable *score* in the Observe window. Choose **Step Into** from the **Run** menu. Note that only one of the *writeln* statements gets executed, as dictated by the value of *score*. Clear all stop signs from the program before continuing.

4. Experiments with if and case

a. The most common errors that arise from the **if** statement come from improper placement of the semicolon statement separator. Try placing a semicolon after the first **then** in **function** *DetermineScore*. TP simply won't let you. It drops the semicolon to the next line, indicating that the statement part of the **if** statement is empty. This is a perfectly legal Pascal program, but it contains a *logic error*—the project will run, but it won't do what you intended it to do. In this case, the semicolon signals to Pascal that the **if** statement is completed and that there is simply nothing at all for the statement to do if *feelsLikeRain* is *true*. No matter what the value of *feelsLikeRain* is, the **if** statement does nothing. It is generally incorrect to put a semicolon after the word **then**.

b. Insert a semicolon after the statement *barRising* := *true* in **procedure** *AskQuestions* and try rerunning the project. This program won't run improperly—in fact, it won't run at all. It contains a *syntax error*. That is, it violates one of Pascal's grammar rules. It is always illegal to put a semicolon before the word **else**.

c. Place a stop sign before the **case** statement in **procedure** *MakePrediction*. Run the project until it stops at this sign. Check the Observe window for the value of variable *score*.

Open the Instant window. Type in the statement *score* := 10; and then click **Do It**. Make sure the value of *score* changes in the Observe window. Then, click **Go** to resume execution.

The project produces a *run-time error*—one that causes no prediction to be displayed. In this example, the error is the result of a **case** statement in which none of its cases has been matched. Although Standard Pascal does not include this feature as part of its definition, TP allows for a **case** statement to be augmented with an **otherwise** clause. When an **otherwise** clause is included with a **case** statement, run-time errors like these are precluded. When none of the branches of a case is matched, the statement of the **otherwise** clause is executed, and no error is reported.

Modify the **case** statement in *MakePrediction* as shown and rerun the project.

```
case score of
    -2, -1, 0:
        writeln('No chance of rain . . . put the top down!');
    1, 2:
        writeln('Slight chance of rain . . . save your rain check.');
    3, 4:
        writeln('Good chance of rain . . . bring your umbrella.');
    5:
        writeln('Major storm coming . . . build an ark!');
    otherwise
        writeln('Score out of range . . . I give up!')
end;
```

5. Safe Programming

A common use for the **if** statement is as a *guard condition*, to catch error conditions and deal with them gracefully before they cause a project to crash. In fact, the above error situation with the **case** statement in *MakePrediction* could be handled without resorting to an **otherwise** clause. You could, for example, have placed an **if..else** around the **case** statement to guard it against an inappropriate value of *score*:

```
if (                          ) then    {You fill in the needed boolean expression.}
    writeln('Score out of range . . . I give up!')
else
    case score of . . .
```

6. Making New Decisions

The predictive skill of the *Weather* program can be expanded to incorporate any evidence whatever. Your intuition is probably as valuable to meteorologists as ours is. Try expanding the program to account for an increase in wind, as follows.

a. Create a new boolean variable named *windIncreased*.

b. Modify *AskQuestions* to solicit a yes-or-no answer to the question, "Has the wind recently increased?".

c. Modify *DetermineScore* to

    i. Add 3 to *score* when the wind has increased, the barometer is falling, and rain is predicted, and

    ii. Subtract 2 from *score* if the wind has increased, the barometer is rising, and it is raining.

d. Adjust the **case** statement in *MakePrediction* to account for a wider range of scores.

Rehash

- TP's Stop Signs allow you to interrupt processing of a project at a specific instruction in a program for debugging purposes.
- The **Stops In** item in the **Debug** menu is a *toggle*, which is to say, an item that is switched to another state (on or off) each time it is selected. When the item is turned on, a check mark appears next to the name, and the left margin of the Program window is outlined, allowing you to place stop signs (called *breakpoints* in technical terms) at any line in the program.

  When the **Stops In** item is not checked, all Stop Signs are removed from the program, though they can be restored to their original positions by selecting the menu item again and checking the item.
- The **Pull Stops** item removes all stops from a program. Unlike **Stops In**, Stop Signs removed using **Pull Stops** are lost for good.
- When stops are enabled, program execution will halt whenever it encounters a stop sign. After that, you may resume execution by using **Go** or either of the **Step** commands from the **Run** menu.

- You may enter any Pascal expression you wish in the Observe window, and that expression will be evaluated when the program halts execution. The expression must be one that could be evaluated by a statement at the location where the program halted. In other words, TP cannot evaluate an expression in the Observe window that uses a variable that is local to a procedure, unless TP is halted within that procedure.

Post-Lab Exercises

1. Extend the PIP as was done in Lab Exercise 6 to do more extensive prediction.
2. Change **procedure** *AskQuestions* to return an additional boolean value as a parameter, named *responsesOK*. *AskQuestions* will set *responsesOK* to *true* only if legal responses are entered for every question asked of the user. If any of the responses is inappropriate to any question, *responsesOK* is set to *false*, and the main program should display a message indicating that no forecasting was attempted, and then quit.

5

Do It Again, and Again: for, while, and repeat Loops

L A B O R A T O R Y

Introduction

The PIP for this chapter is interesting not only because it solves a problem using sophisticated numerical techniques but also because it does so using Pascal loops. The program, *TrapezoidTest*, was written both to calculate an approximate value for the constant π and to illustrate all three of Pascal's standard looping statements—**for**, **while**, and **repeat**. These iterative control structures allow groups of statements within the program to be executed over and over again, either a fixed number of times or subject to the value of some conditional expression. Iteration completes your basic repertoire of Pascal statements and allows you to express virtually any well-defined algorithm as a Pascal program.

Because of the power that these statements afford us, their semantics—how they do what they do—are complex and require careful analysis. In this lab, we will apply all that we know about TP's debugging and analysis tools to the task of understanding Pascal's loops.

L A B   O B J E C T I V E S

In this lab, we will:

- Help you to analyze and understand the Chapter 5 PIP, *TrapezoidTest*.
- Illustrate and guide you in experimenting with Pascal **for**, **while**, and **repeat** statements.
- Show you how to avoid some common loop-oriented mistakes.
- Help you to alter and extend the PIP to incorporate some additional iterative statements.

Exercises

1. Running *TrapezoidTest*

If you have not already done so, review the section of the Chapter 5 text that describes the PIP in detail before going on. Add the Lab 5 program to your generic project.

a. Run the project a few times, providing different values for the number of intervals. Convince yourself that the approximations to π are indeed more accurate with more intervals. How many intervals do you need to get an approximation that is accurate to two decimal places (that is, an approximation that would round to 3.14)? How many intervals do you need to get four-place accuracy (that is, 3.1416)?

b. Make sure that *TrapezoidTest*'s Program window is active. Then, set stop signs at the following locations:

   i. At the **end** statement in **function** *Trapezoid* just before the line *Trapezoid := sum*.

   ii. At the line *Trapezoid := sum*.

   iii. At the **while** statement in **function** *ReadyToQuit*.

   iv. At the **until** clause in the main program.

c. Now open the Observe window and enter the following expressions into it: *n, i, lowx, highx, sum, f(lowx), f(highx)*, and *ans*. As we did before, move the windows around and size them so that none overlap.

2. Watching and Watching and Watching Loops

We are now set up to watch the processing of *TrapezoidTest*'s loops in full detail. Rerun the project now, until it stops at the first stop sign. Use a small number for *n*, like 5, to avoid boredom while stepping through the **for** loop.

a. The program should now be in **function** *Trapezoid*. The value of parameter *n* should be that which you entered as the desired number of iterations.

Step through the loop a few times one instruction at a time, watching the values of *i, lowx, highx*, and *sum* as they change with each iteration. Use **Step Over** to avoid diving into the **function** *f*.

b. Choose **Go**, as often as needed, to continue execution to the next stop sign, the one after the **for** loop in *Trapezoid*. Notice the value of control variable *i* at this point. It should be the same as the value of *n*, since that was the value *i* had when it was last tested in the loop. That's what happens in TP, but it's not necessarily so with other compilers. Never assume you can predict the value of the index variable when a **for** loop quits.

c. Now, choose **Go** again until you get to **function** *ReadyToQuit*. At this point, you have just been asked to enter a value for variable *ans* in response to the question, "Do you wish to run the program again?" Type the character 'z'. Make sure *ans* shows its value in the Observe window.

Before stepping through the **while** loop, enter the loop's condition as an expression in the Observe window. Go ahead, type

(ans <> 'Y') **and** (ans <> 'y') **and** (ans <> 'N') **and** (ans <> 'n')

into the next available slot.

Now step through the loop one instruction at a time. It should give you another chance to enter a legal response. Enter 'y' (or 'Y'), hit Return, and choose **Go** to execute, at last, to the stop sign in the main program.

d. Since you entered 'y' for *ans*, the **function** *ReadyToQuit* should have returned the value *false*, and the main program should repeat the main loop again.

Choose **Step Over** enough times to convince yourself that the main program will indeed repeat. When you are prompted to enter another value for the number of intervals, click the "bug spray" can to interrupt execution.

Now choose **Pull Stops** from the **Debug** menu to remove all stop signs from your program before continuing.

3. Common Loop Errors

a. Notice that there is no semicolon after the word **do** in any of our loops. Change the **for** loop in **function** *Trapezoid* by placing a semicolon immediately after the **do**. Now run the program. What happens?

The **for** statement is a compound statement, one that includes another statement within it. The syntax of a **for** statement is such that the Pascal compiler expects **do** (in either a **for** or **while** loop) to be followed by a statement (or group of statements), so that

```
for i : = 0 to n − 1 do
  ;     {Do the following for each trapezoid . . .}
begin   {Compute the area of each trapezoid and add it to the running sum.}
  lowx : = lower + i * delta;
    ⋮
end;
```

would be requesting Pascal to perform the *empty statement* between the **do** and the semicolon *n* times, after which the group of statements beginning with *lowx := lower + i * delta* would be performed (once!).

Take the semicolon out to restore the program to its original state.

b. What happens if you try to modify the value of the control variable while a **for** loop is executing? Try this by including $i := i - 1$ within the **begin..end** block in *Trapezoid*'s **for** loop. What happens?

You'll have to click the "bug spray" can, because the program was stuck in the **for** loop. The loop never got to the limit value $n - 1$, because every time the **for** statement increased i by one, the statement $i := i - 1$ set it back to zero. You can see this by putting a stop at the **end** of the loop and observing the value of i.

Well, well, well. We've just discovered that TP is a wee bit lazy, since according to the standard it is an error to modify the value of the control variable within a **for** loop. Technically speaking, TP isn't violating the standard here, since the meaning of *error* is "a violation of the standard that is allowed to pass undetected." We'll just have to remember that TP won't tell us when we've erred, but other compilers might.

Take out the offending statement.

c. Now change your version of **function** *Trapezoid* so that it includes the statement $n := 2 * n$ in the body of its **for** loop. Before you run this, try to guess what will happen.

Now try running this program with input 5. Notice that n begins with value 5 and then is repeatedly doubled to become 10, 20, 40, 80, and 160; but the loop still iterates five times. The moral is, you can modify the limits of a **for** loop, but that will not affect the number of loop iterations.

4. A Loop Is a Loop Is a Loop

We mention in the text that any iteration can be accomplished in a variety of ways. For example, the lower and upper limits of a **for** loop (which prescribe the number of times the loop is to be performed) can be specified in almost any way, as long as the statements of the loop take it into account. Also, **for** loops can either move "up" from a lower limit "to" an upper limit, or "down to" a lower limit from an upper limit. Finally, **while** loops and **repeat** loops can be interchanged by reorganizing the loops and negating their logical conditions. Exploring these alternative methods will help you to understand both the similarities and the differences among these forms of iteration.

a. Look again at the **for** loop in **function** *Trapezoid*. Try changing the loop so that its control variable starts with value $n - 1$ and moves **downto** 0. Will you have to modify the statements in the loop to reflect the change in i?

b. The **for** loop in **function** *Trapezoid* could be modified even more dramatically and still produce the same results. The control variable, i, ranges from 0 to $n - 1$ (counting n repetitions) and is used directly in the calculations of *lowx* and *highx*. Change the loop so that i ranges from 1 to n (still counting n repetitions). What changes will you have to make to the statements in the loop?

Make them now and convince yourself that the program results are identical to those of the original.

c. Now, examine the **while** loop in **function** *ReadyToQuit*. It conforms to the standard format for a **while** loop, in that it reads a controlling value before starting the loop; immediately checks to see if the loop should be executed; and, if so, reads a controlling value at the end of the loop before trying again. What is the logical negation of the loop's condition?

Use this expression to rewrite the **while** loop using **repeat..until**. (It need not behave precisely like the original, but it shouldn't ask any superfluous questions!)

d. Rewrite the **repeat..until** loop in the main program as a **while** loop. The result will be a bit longer than the original but will perform the same. Now you should be able to see why we used the loop structures we did.

5. Extending the PIP

Let's try incorporating two further extensions into your version of *Trapezoid-Test* that will provide you with further loop experience.

a. In its current state, an input of zero for the number of intervals (n, in the main program), produces a meaningless message to the effect that the approximate value of π is zero. Trace through the program now, entering zero as input, to explain why.

Digression: Notice, by the way, that we're not getting an error message when we should. If n is zero, the statement $delta := (upper - lower) / n$ should be meaningless, since we can't divide by zero. This is another error, but it's one you can tell TP to catch. Look at the Project window and notice the letters D, N, V, and R to the left of the program name. Clicking on any of these toggles them on or off. If a letter is boxed, it means that a particular kind of error checking is enabled. The meanings of these error checks are:

D: General debugging. Without it, you get no notice of where an error occurred or what it was.

N: Inserts names into the compiled code. Don't worry about this one.

V: Overflow checks on. This catches division by zero.

R: Range checks on. This will inform you, for example, that an integer calculation has exceeded *maxint*.

So much for the digression. Modify the program by adding an input procedure that prompts the user for an input repeatedly until the user enters a positive integer. Look at *ReadyToQuit* for an idea.

b. Finally, change the loop in the main program (and add whatever statements you think are necessary) to regard an input of zero as a sentinel value. That is, an input of zero should signal to the program that no further runs are desired and that processing should terminate. You can choose from many alternate methods for accomplishing this. For example, you can revise the main program to eliminate reference to *ReadyToQuit* or change the body of *ReadyToQuit*.

Rehash

- Stop signs and stepping are particularly useful in analyzing the behavior of a loop, especially when combined with observing the value of the exit condition of the loop.
- In TP, the value of the control variable of a **for** loop upon exit from the loop will be the last value tested. In other words, in a **for..to** loop, the exit value of the control variable will be the value after the upper limit, and in a **for..downto** loop, the exit value of the control variable will be the value just prior to the lower limit value.
- TP handles the error of modifying the control variable of a **for** loop by not reporting it.
- TP allows the programmer to specify the amount of error-checking in a program by setting toggles in the Project window. D performs general debugging (and should be left on until you're sure the program is bug-free), V tests for arithmetic overflow (like division by zero), and R tests for range errors (about which we'll see much more in Chapters 8 and 9). Turning these on instructs TP to insert error-checking code into the compiled program — and thus makes the compiled code somewhat longer. Generally speaking, it's good policy to turn all three on (indicated by boxes around the letters) and leave them that way.

Post-Lab Exercises

1. Notice that, in the original version of **function** *Trapezoid*, the values *lowx* and *highx* are each essentially incremented by *delta* with each pass through the function's **for** loop. In fact, after each iteration, *lowx* takes on what was the previous value for *highx*, thus eliminating the need for recalculating either *lowx* or *f(lowx)*—which is equal to the value of *f(highx)* from the previous iteration. Revise the loop to avoid these redundant calculations.

2. Write a program that implements Newton's iterative technique for approximating square roots. The program should read a real value from the user and should make an initial guess that the square root of the input is the input itself. Successive guesses can be generated as:

   guess := (sqr(guess) + input) / (2.0 * guess)

   The program should continue making guesses until the absolute value of the difference between the square of the guess and the original input is less than some prescribed accuracy, like $1e-5$.

3. Do Exercise 30 in Chapter 5 of the text.

Text Processing: Characters, Strings, and Keyboard I/O

L A B O R A T O R Y

Introduction

The two programs that compose this chapter's PIP demonstrate virtually all of Pascal's built-in facilities for manipulating text. The programs, which encode and then decode messages using a Caesar cypher, illustrate how data in character form (*char* and **string**) are read, stored, accessed, manipulated, and written. They also give hints as to how these text-processing operations can be applied to almost any program. In this lab, we will review how textual data is processed by our PIPs, *EncryptCaesar* and *DecryptCaesar*, expand the programs to do more sophisticated analyses, and apply the same techniques to other problems and programs.

L A B   O B J E C T I V E S

In this lab, we will:

- Run and review the PIPs for this chapter.
- Analyze text-processing operations in the PIPs, using TP's debugging facilities.
- Use Pascal's character-manipulation operations to improve the PIPs' input checking.
- Extend the PIPs to produce more sophisticated output and to perform additional analyses.

Exercises

1. Decoding the PIPs

Before attempting to analyze or extend the PIPs, you should run them both a few times to get a feeling for how they work. Notice, there are two programs in the Chapter 6 folder of your Pascal's Triangle disk. Of course, you'll add them to your project one at a time, since we know a project can have only one program.

a. Run the *EncryptCaesar* program first, in the by-now familiar way. You will be asked to provide an integer offset to be used in encoding a message, and then you will be prompted for a string to be encoded. Enter a string, followed by a Return, and the program will produce the encoded version.

Run the project a few more times, recording your input message and its encoded form each time. Then replace *EncryptCaesar* in your project with the *DecryptCaesar* program.

b. Now run the *DecryptCaesar* program. When prompted for input here, enter one of the outputs from the encryption program. Choose any "most likely character" (try 'e', for example) when asked to, and see if the program correctly decodes the original message. If it doesn't, try again with another choice of most likely character. A good choice, of course, would be the most likely character of your input message.

Run the *DecryptCaesar* project on all of the strings produced by the *EncryptCaesar* program until each is successfully decoded.

2. The Details of Encryption/Decryption

We can now take advantage of TP's analysis and debugging facilities to slow down and make clear the process of encoding and decoding strings. As you would expect, we will focus our analysis on the *char* and **string** manipulations that are being performed. Load *EncryptCaeser* into your project.

a. We'll look at **function** *Cap* first. Insert a stop sign at the line $Cap := chr(ord(ch) - ord('a') + ord('A'))$ and then enter the following expressions in the Observe window:

```
ch
ord(ch)
 - ord('a') + ord('A')
chr(ord(ch) - ord('a') + ord('A'))
```

Run *EncryptCaesar*, using an offset of 8 and input string 'Try it out!'. In your own words, how does *Cap* capitalize a lowercase letter?

b. Now let's look at *ConvertToCapAlpha*. Remove the stop sign you had before (which you can do by dragging it from the margin) and place three stops in

ConvertToCapAlpha: at the top **if** statement and at the two internal **ends**. Enter the following expressions in the Observe window:

s

i

s[i]

i

t

Run the program, using the same offset and string as before. What happens to the nonalphabetic characters (the two blanks and the exclamation point)?

c. Finally, let's look at the **procedure** *CaesarCypher*. Remove the stops you had before (**Pull Stops** is probably easier than dragging in this case) and place a stop at the statement in the **for** loop that begins *outStr[i]* := .... Enter the following expressions in the Observe window (it'll save typing if you **Copy** and **Paste** diligently):

instr

outstr

outstr[i]

ord(outstr[i]) − ord('A')

ord(outstr[i]) − ord('A') + offset

(ord(outstr[i]) − ord('A') + offset) **mod** 26

chr(ord('A') + (ord(outstr[i]) − ord('A') + offset) **mod** 26)

Run the program, using the same offset and string as before. Notice that with an offset of 8, the 'I' gets shifted eight letters forward to 'Q'. Make sure you understand how letters get wrapped around the alphabet. Quick, what would 'X' get converted to?

3. Safer I/O

We have, in previous labs, taken a variety of measures to improve our programs' handling of user-provided input, all in the interest of ensuring that the program operate on legitimate values. Still, what we have seen to date is lacking. For example, if a program expects an integer as input, but the user enters a non-integer value, any of the programs we have seen so far would be at a loss. (In fact, TP handles such errors for us by informing the user that an inappropriate value has been entered and then shutting the program down.) Another step along the road to controlling user input is to do, in essence, what TP now does for us: that is, read all data in as characters (or strings)—in which case anything that can be typed from the keyboard conforms type-wise—and then attempt to convert the character representation to a value of the expected type.

a. The *EncryptCaesar* program expects a user to enter an integer offset to be used in encoding the message. Let's write a *GetOffset* function of the following form:

```
function GetOffset: integer;
{Reads a value in string form and converts it to an integer.}
var
    StrInt: string;
    value, i : integer;
begin
    write('Offset to be used in encryption? ');
    readln(strInt);
    value := 0;
    for i := 1 to Length(strInt) do
        if ('0' <= strInt[i]) and (strInt[i] <= '9') then    {got a good character}
            value := 10 * value + (ord(strInt[i]) − ord('0'))
        else                                            {Error. A nondigit was seen.}
            writeln('Sorry. The input must be an integer.');
    GetOffset := value
end;
```

b. Now let's inspect this function more carefully. If you've looked at the text, you'll recognize that the expression $ord(strInt[i]) − ord('0')$ computes the integer equivalent of the digit character $strInt[i]$, so that the character '3' yields the integer 3. How does this function change the string '123' into the integer 123, though?

Try it: Write *GetOffset* and call it in the main program where the program gets the offset. Put a stop at the **for** statement, enter the string '123' at the prompt, and use the Observe window while you step through the loop to inspect the successive values of *value*. What happens?

c. Try this with the illegal input '12r4' (Oops! the user's finger slipped). What is the value returned by the function?

d. This isn't a very satisfactory function, since the **for** loop continues processing characters even if an error is seen. Using what you learned in Chapter 5, try to replace the **for** loop with a **while** loop that stops processing input as soon as a nondigit character is encountered.

4. Cracking the Codes

The operation of *DecryptCaesar* should not be too mysterious to you, in that many of the subprograms it uses are precisely those used to encode messages. The most notable exceptions are the main program and the *GuessSolution* procedure.

The main program in *DecryptCaesar* asks the user to provide a candidate for the most likely character found in the original English message. That character is then mapped to the most frequently occurring character in the encoded message. This allows the *GuessSolution* procedure to make an educated guess at the offset used to encode the message. *GuessSolution* reverses the offset (using $26 - offset$) to retrieve the original message.

a. Asking the user to provide a most likely character is somewhat unrealistic. A better approach would be for the program to use the fact that E, T, A, O, N, and I are, in order, the most common letters in English text — and produce decoded versions using each of these characters as the key to the offset. Revise your *DecryptCaesar* program to produce the six most likely decodings of the input message automatically.

b. Another similar approach to decoding Caesar cypher messages is not to do it at all! That is, instead of having a program produce what it "thinks" might be plausible decodings of a message, have the program produce data that will help a human analyst to accomplish the decoding.

What would be helpful to a human analyst in this case? Human analysts know the relative frequencies of all 26 letters in English text. Let's modify our program to produce analogous frequency data for its encoded message and let the human do the analysis. We'll do this in two stages.

i. Modify your *DecryptCaesar* program so that before it displays its six best guesses, it displays the number of occurrences of each of the 26 alphabetic characters in the encoded message.

ii. Now, revise the program so that the frequency data for the 26 characters is displayed as a simple *histogram*:

```
A    ******
B    **
C    ***
D
E    *
F    ****
     ⋮
Z    **
```

Rehash

- Don't forget, strings are an extension to Pascal and are not part of the standard. This means that you can't assume that a program that uses strings will work on all compilers. Even compilers that use strings may have different string-handling subprograms, so be careful.

Post-Lab Exercises

1. Rewrite the *DecryptCaesar* program to base its decoding on the most common English digrams (letter pairs), as opposed to merely the most common single letters. The six most frequent adjacent letter pairs in English text are, in descending order, *TH*, *IN*, *ER*, *RE*, *AN*, and *HE*.
2. Write a pair of programs similar to *EncryptCaesar* and *DecryptCaesar* that accomplish encoding and decoding of messages using the "railfence" technique described in Chapter 6 of your text.
3. Write a program that reads a sequence of lines of text from the keyboard and then counts and displays the number of words entered.

Subprograms Revisited:
Parameters, Scope, and Recursion

Introduction

You've made considerable use of functions and procedures so far. To avoid confusing you with a mass of detail, though, we've left out some explanations of the detailed workings of subprograms. Now that you have subprograms pretty much in hand, we'll use this lab to fill in the gaps in our exposition, using as our example a PIP that uses the technique of *recursive descent* to determine whether an input string is a legal Pascal identifier.

L AB OBJECTIVES

In this lab, we will:

- Demonstrate how TP units are defined and accessed.
- Review in detail the operation of this chapter's PIP, *IDTester*.
- Conduct a series of experiments to illustrate the concepts of scope, local and global variables, and parameter passing.
- Use the PIP to demonstrate the behavior of a recursive procedure.
- Help you to extend the *IDTester* program to recognize other Pascal syntactic objects.

Exercises

1. Using TP Units

The PIP 7 folder contains a project we've made for you, along with two other files. When you open project *IDTester.π* you will notice something different about it. The project contains, in addition to the standard runtime and interface libraries and the *IDTester* program itself, something else. This something else is *StartFinish*, a **unit**: a collection of type, variable, and subprogram declarations that may be included in any project. Double-click on *StartFinish* in the Project window to open the unit and display it in a TP window.

As you can see, *StartFinish* looks something like (although not exactly like) a Pascal program. The main differences are: (1) *StartFinish* begins with the designation that it is a unit, not a program; (2) *StartFinish* has no main program segment after its declarations — and so cannot be executed on its own; and (3) *StartFinish* has two distinct subsections, an **interface** part (in this case, a function header) and an **implementation** part, containing the body of the function with an abbreviated header.

This is the general form of a TP unit, and we are free to define our own, just as we write our own programs. Normally, units are defined to group collections of related declarations together and to make them available to other programs. The **interface** part of a unit shows other programs and units what is accessible to them (in this case, the function named *NegativeAnswerTo* and the *Setup* procedure. The **implementation** part hides from other programs and units the details of how *NegativeAnswerTo* and *Setup* are implemented.

a. To use a unit, a program (or another unit) must include a **uses** clause at the beginning of its declaration section, as does *IDTester*. Programs can use as many units as they wish, as long as each is included in the program's uses clause and the units themselves are included in the running project. Notice that the unit being referenced, *StartFinish*, is listed before the program that references it, *IDTester*, in the Project window. This is important to the compiler.

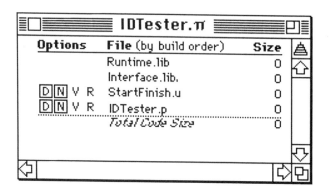

Move the mouse to the Project window. Click and drag the unit named *StartFinish* until it appears below the *IDTester* entry in the Project window. This is how units and programs can be reordered within a project.

Now, choose **Build** from the **Run** menu to try to rebuild this project. The error message tells you that the pieces of this project are out of order. Drag *IDTester* below *StartFinish* in the Project window, and the project can be rebuilt and run.

b. Notice, too, that the main program calls **procedure** *Setup* and **function** *NegativeAnswerTo*, even though the subprograms do not appear in *IDTester*. When TP can't locate a reference in the current program, it searches in the units listed in the **uses** clause to find its declaration.

Remove the **uses** clause from *IDTester* and try to run the project. Now TP cannot find the **procedure** *Setup*, so it sends an error message. Replace the **uses** clause after reading and understanding the error message that resulted.

2. Parsing in Action

Now that your version of *IDTester* is back in working order, run it. Enter a variety of strings as input, and the program will correctly distinguish legal Pascal identifiers from illegal ones.

a. Or will it? Try a very long, but legal, input like

gkujfd98tr9fterqfgifrqterfgvoryt8re76587f74357f486gvjvbiry95469876

If your input was long enough, you probably got an error message about insufficient stack space. This is because *IDTester* makes a lot of procedure calls on a long input, and many of these calls have to wait for subsequent ones before the subprogram returns. A pending subprogram call requires some information to be stored temporarily. All of this information is stored in a chunk of memory called the *stack*, and you just ran over the available stack space. To fix this problem, TP allows you to specify the stack size.

Go to the **Run** menu and select the **Run Options** item. A dialog box will appear, and near the bottom you'll find a **Stack Size** box with a number in it, like 16. This means that TP has set aside 16K bytes (K is a binary thousand, equal to 1024) for the stack. Type a larger number, like 256, in the box to allocate more stack room; click the **OK** button; and run the program again with a large input. Things should go just fine now.

b. Now let's watch the program in slow motion. In Lab 6, we looked at the PIP from the bottom up; here, we'll work from the top down, by first analyzing *IsAnID*. Put a stop at the first **begin** in *IsAnID* and enter the following expressions in the Observe window:

```
s
s[1]
Tail(s)
NoBadChars(Tail(s))
IsALetter(s[1])
```

Now run the program on the legal input 'u8_it.' Notice that both *NoBad-Chars(Tail(s))* and *IsALetter(s[1])* are *true*, so 'u8_it.' is a legal identifier (its first character is a letter, and there are no bad characters following the first). Try the same thing with the illegal identifiers 'me?' and '2bad'. Record the values of *IsALetter(s[1])* and *NoBadChars(Tail(s))* to see how *IsAnID* works.

c. The recursive part of the program is the **function** *NoBadChars*. Let's see how it works. Put another stop in, at the first **begin** of *NoBadChars*, and include in the Observe window the expressions *IsADigit(s[1])* and *IsAn-Underscore(s[1])*. Run the program on the three inputs above and notice how *NoBadChars* nibbles away at the input string by successively calling itself on smaller and smaller copies of the string *s*.

How many times does *NoBadChars* get called for each input string? What is the relationship between the number of times *NoBadChars* calls itself and the length of the input string?

d. What happens if we remove the exit case from a recursive subprogram? Let's find out by removing the first **if** from *NoBadChars*, so that it begins **if** *IsALetter(s[1])*. . . . Run the program on a legal input. What happened? To give you a clue, try running the damaged program with and without the R box for *IDTester* checked in the Project window, and remember that R checks that a number is in an allowable range. Try inserting a statement *writeln* ('Current character is ', *s[1]*) at the start of *NoBadChars* to help you see what's happening.

3. The Need to Know: Scope

We have been careful in **program** *IDTester* to take advantage of Pascal's facility for defining information like parameters and variables on a "need to know" basis. That is, both subprograms and data are defined as locally as possible to allow them to do their jobs. Try making the following changes to **program** *IDTester*. In each case, write down what happens when you try to run the resulting project and do your best to explain TP's reaction. (*Note:* To avoid permanently deranging your program, select the **Don't Save** option from the **Run** menu. This will cause any changes you make to be made on the working copy of your program in memory, and not on the version saved on the disk.)

a. Call *IsAnID* from *IDTester*'s main program (by including the statement **if** *IsAnID*(*testString*) **then** *writeln*('OK')).

b. Call *IsAnID* from *SolicitInput* (by including the statement **if** *IsAnID*(*test-String*) **then** *writeln*('OK')).

c. Call *IsADigit* from *IsALetter* (by including the statement **if** *IsADigit*(*c*) **then** *writeln*('OK')).

d. Call *IsALetter* from *IsADigit* (by including the statement **if** *IsALetter*(*c*) **then** *writeln*(*c*, ' is a letter.')).

e. Add the statement *writeln*('Current s string is: ', *s*) in the main program.

Now, review your experiences above in light of the block structure of **program** *IDTester* (refer to the text for a diagram, if you wish). If you understand why TP performed as it did in each of these cases, you have a pretty good understanding of Pascal's scope rules.

4. Extending the Parser

We have made the point in passing that one of the virtues of organizing a program as we have organized *IDTester* is its extensibility. We'll do our best to demonstrate that to you now, as we ask you to extend the parser, one subprogram at a time. Our goal is that, by the end of this lab, your version of *IDTester* will recognize Pascal strings and integers, in addition to the identifiers it already handles so gracefully. Our approach will be both incremental and bottom-up, so do the following exercises in the order prescribed.

a. Add a function declaration to *TestAString* with heading **function** *IsACharacter*(*c*: *char*): *boolean*. The function should return *true* or *false* to indicate whether or not its input parameter is a legal Pascal string character (that is, if its ASCII code is in the range 32–126 — excluding 39, the code for the single quote).

b. Now, write a **function** *IsCharacters*(*s*: **string**): *boolean* that uses *IsACharacter* to determine if an entire string is made up solely of string characters. This can be written iteratively — looping character-by-character through the input string — or recursively (use *NoBadChars* as a model for a simple recursive version).

c. A Pascal string is, by definition, a (possibly empty) sequence of string characters surrounded by single quotes. Use **function** *IsCharacters*, above, to write another new **function** *IsString* (*s*: **string**): *boolean*. Modify the *IDTester* program so that if a particular input string is not a legal identifier, the program checks to see if it is a legal Pascal string.

d. Use the following information to extend your parser to recognize Pascal integers:

A Pascal integer is a signed integer.
A signed integer is a sign followed by an unsigned integer.
A sign is a '+' or a '−'.
An unsigned integer is a digit sequence.
A digit sequence is a string containing only digits.

You already have a function named *IsADigit*. Start from there, using it to define other functions until you have declared **function** *IsAnInteger*(*s*: **string**): *boolean*.

Now, modify your program so that it uses *IsAnInteger*. The final version of *IDTester* should effectively distinguish Pascal identifiers, strings, and integers from one another and should recognize when a given input conforms to none of these formats. By the way, these syntactic classes are disjoint; that is, no input can conform to more than one of these formats.

Rehash

- A TP project may contain only one program, but it can have as many units as needed. A unit is defined like a program, except that it has no statement body and consists only of constant, type, variable, and subprogram declarations.
- The **interface** part of a unit contains constant, type, and variable declarations, and subprogram headers. These are available to any unit or program that **uses** the unit.
- The **implementation** part of a unit contains declarations and the non-header parts of subprograms, none of which are available outside the unit.
- In TP, the stack space available to a program for storing information about pending subprogram calls may be set by using the **Run Options** command from the **Run** menu.

- A very useful debugging technique is to include *diagnostic code*, which displays the current state of a variable or expression, such as *writeln* ('Current character is ', $s[1]$).

Post-Lab Exercises

1. Look up the syntax diagram for *real numbers* in your TP manual or in the text. Use it to help you define a collection of subprograms that can be added to your parser to allow it to recognize Pascal real numbers.
2. Return to the PIPs from Chapter 6, *EncryptCaesar* and *DecryptCaesar*. These two separate programs use many of the same subprograms. Identify which subprograms are common to the two programs and define a unit, named *Cryptic*, to hold them. Then, modify the two programs so that each uses **unit** *Cryptic*.

8 From Algorithms to Data Structures: User-Defined Types

L A B O R A T O R Y

Introduction

The topics introduced in this chapter of the text are basically extensions to the Pascal language. That is, they are features above and beyond more conventional control and data structures, added primarily to improve program readability. It is not that as a result of reading the text chapter and doing these lab exercises you will be able to program anything you couldn't have before; rather, these extensions will allow you to do some of what you've already done a little more directly and at a higher level.

The emphasis, then, in this lab will be on programmer and user convenience. The lab begins with the concept of a user-defined type and will go on to introduce you to Pascal subranges, sets, and enumerated types. The PIP for this chapter is one that you've already seen (*Zeller*, from Chapter 1), revised to exploit these new extensions.

L A B   O B J E C T I V E S

In this lab, we will:

- Review the PIPs as an illustration of Pascal subranges and sets.
- Use Pascal subranges as a means for checking user input to **program** *ImprovedZeller*.
- Use Pascal **sets** to develop an improved routine for soliciting and checking user-provided input.

Exercises

1. *Zeller,* Again

We've spruced up *Zeller* by using subrange types and sets. With the Pascal expertise you've gained so far, it should be much more comprehensible than it was when you first encountered it. First, run the *ImprovedZeller* program (we're back to using your generic project here) with current dates or with dates for which you know the corresponding day of the week. Don't turn on range checking; that is, make sure the R in the Project window is not boxed. Then, we'll examine the features that have been added to render the program more intelligible.

    a. Run the project again, using the following as input: 32 14 1900. What does the program do? We don't need to remind you that there's no 14th month and that no month has 32 days, do we?

    b. Set a stop sign at the final *write* statement of the main program. Run the project to the stop sign with a valid date and then open the Instant window.
        Enter the statement *weekDay* : = 33; in the Instant window and click **Do It**. Then, continue running the project. What does the program do now?

2. Range Checking in TP

Both of the above events violate the data declarations of **program** *Improved-Zeller*. The main program reads values of 14 for *month*, even though it was declared as 1 .. 12, and 32 for *day*, which was declared to be of **type** 1 .. 31. However, these values don't stop the program from attempting to determine on what day of the week the 32nd day of the 14th month of 1900 occurred.

In part 1b, the blatant assignment of 33 to variable *weekDay*, which is declared to be of **type** 0 .. 6 is allowed, but causes the **case** statement in **procedure** *WriteDay* to have no effect.

    a. We said in the text that the most significant advantage of subrange declarations is that they clarify the source listing for human readers. At this point, such declarations do little to excite TP, since we haven't told it to catch such errors. As we saw earlier, that's easy enough to fix—all we have to do is enable range checking. Do so now, by checking the R box next to *Improved-Zeller.p* in the Project window.

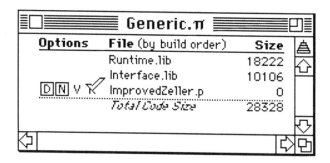

b. Now, rerun the above experiments. Notice that each produces a fatal error.

3. New, Improved I/O

By enlisting TP's help in performing run-time range checking, we have improved the program, in the sense that it doesn't blindly plow ahead when given (or internally generating) meaningless data. The bad news is that when TP detects a subrange violation, it regards this condition as a fatal run-time error and aborts execution of the program.

a. In the text we describe an alternative strategy that represents a modest improvement. The approach, outlined in Section 8.6, is to declare all of the variables that are currently declared as subranges of the integers (that is, *day*, *month*, *adjMonth*, *weekDay*) as full-blown integers. Then, include your own range-checking code to make sure, for example, that a value entered for *month* is in the range 1 .. 12. Fill in the details of **procedure** *GetDate*:

```
procedure GetDate(var day: DayRange; var month: MonthRange; var year: integer);
var
    d, m, y : integer;
begin
    writeln('At the prompt, enter numbers for day, month, and year.');
    write('>');
    readln(d, m, y);
    {You fill in the rest.}




    day : = d;
    month : = m;
    year : = y
end;
```

b. Revise your main program to use *GetDate* now. Rerun your program, leaving TP's range checking on, to convince yourself that your new input checker works.

4. The Ultimate Prompter

One of the other extensions introduced into *ImprovedZeller* is the use of sets in a revised version of the *NegativeAnswerTo* function from Lab 7. Notice how *NegativeAnswerTo* defines a local set, *goodResponses*, to contain the collection of single characters that constitute legitimate responses to the question the function presents.

a. Set a stop sign at the **while** statement in *NegativeAnswerTo* and enter *resp* **in** *goodResponses* into the Observe window. Run the program to the stop sign.

You have just entered a value for *resp* that should give a value to the above expression. This value tells you—and TP—whether or not to enter the loop. Enter a few responses that are not "good" and watch what happens.

b. We've said several times that it's often a good idea to make subprograms as general as is conveniently possible. Let's redesign *NegativeAnswerTo* so that it serves to get general character answers. What we have in mind is a function like this:

function *AnswerTo:*

IN: *message* (a **string**), which will be displayed as a prompt to the user.
goodResponses (a **set of** *char*), which will consist of all the valid responses to the prompt message.
numberTries (an *integer*), which specifies the number of invalid responses the operator will be allowed.
defaultResponse (a *char*), which will be returned if the user makes more than *numberTries* invalid responses.

OUT: the first valid response entered by the operator, or the default response (if the operator made too many incorrect responses).

Function *AnswerTo* displays *message* on the screen repeatedly, either until the user enters a single-character response that is in the **set** *goodResponses* or until the function gives up after some *numberTries*. If the function gives up, it will return with the value specified in *defaultResponse*.

Try to write **function** *AnswerTo* now. Test it by using it to replace *NegativeAnswerTo* in *ImprovedZeller*. That is, instead of invoking *NegativeAnswerTo*, call:

r := Prompt('Do you want to run the program again? ', ['n', 'N', 'y', 'Y'], 2, 'n')

Then, modify the main program to do the final check to see if the value *r* returned by prompt is 'N' or 'n'.

(Notice we used 'n' as the default response, rather than 'y'. It's always a good idea to arrange your program so that the user always has a way out of a program, no matter how confused she or he gets. There are few things more frustrating than being locked into a program with no apparent way out.)

Remember, we can't use anonymous types within formal parameter lists, so you'll have to declare a global **type** *ChrSet* = **set of** *char*.

c. Now test your new function. Make sure that you're not off by one in counting the number of tries allowed to the user. Also, did you think to handle the situation where the *numberTries* parameter was negative or zero? You'll have to decide what the Good Thing to do in this situation would be.

d. Once you're convinced it is correct, record your version of **function** *AnswerTo* in a unit of its own. Your unit will have the following format:

unit Prompts;

  interface

    type
      ChrSet: **set of** char;
    function AnswerTo (message: **string**;
                goodResponses: ChrSet;
                numberRetries: integer;
                defaultResponse : char): char;

  implementation

    function AnswerTo; {(message: string;   }
               { goodResponses: ChrSet;   }
               { numberRetries: integer;   }
               { defaultResponse : char): char}
    {YOUR DECLARATIONS AND CODE HERE}
end.

Include the unit in your project, along with a **uses** directive in *Improved-Zeller*, and test it again.

Post-Lab Exercises

1. It would be good to have *AnswerTo* inform the user what the valid responses were, as we did in the original *NegativeAnswerTo*. The problem, though, is that we have no way of knowing ahead of time what the **set** *goodResponses* will contain. What we need is a **procedure** *WriteChrSet*(*s* : *ChrSet*), which will print all and only those characters in the **set** *s*. If we had that, then the loop body of *AnswerTo* could look like this, in part:

```
begin
    writeln('Sorry, that''s not a valid response.');
    writeln('Please enter one of the following characters, then press the Return key:');
    WriteChrSet(goodResponses);
    writeln;
    write(message);
    readln(resp);
    ⋮
end;
```

Modify *AnswerTo* to incorporate these changes.

2. The *IDTester* program from Chapter 7 could be simplified considerably, at least in its low-level details, by using sets — to see if something is a digit, for example. Revise *IDTester* to use Pascal sets.

CHAPTER

9

Homogeneous Data Structures: Arrays

L A B O R A T O R Y

Introduction

Adding arrays to our Pascal arsenal increases our programming range considerably. With arrays we have the ability to store, access, and process large collections of related data in ways that were either impractical or impossible without them. Defining a collection of data items (all of the same type) as an array affords us the luxury of accessing directly elements of the collections (so that, for example, we can read, write, and assign individual values). It also allows us to refer to the array as a whole (for example, as a parameter to a subprogram, or so that it can be assigned to another array).

Our PIP for this chapter exploits the features of arrays in performing the tasks of reading, sorting, and printing lists of numbers. We'll start by using the sorting technique described in the text, the Selection Sort, to illustrate the mechanics of using arrays. Then, consistent with both our programming goals and the CS Interlude for this chapter, we'll incorporate some additional sorting algorithms into our PIP and analyze them for efficiency.

L A B   O B J E C T I V E S

In this lab, we will:

- Enlist TP's debugging tools to help us analyze the use of arrays in our PIP, *Sorter.*
- Add simple counters to the programs, which allow us to analyze the efficiency of the sorting algorithm.

- Review the Quicksort algorithm described in the text, incorporate it into our project, and test it.

Exercises

1. Arrays and Selection Sort

Change your generic project to include the two files in the PIP 9 folder named *Sorter.p* and *Array.u*. Don't forget to place them in the project in the correct order. Turn on range checking (this comes in particularly handy when dealing with arrays and subscripts) and then open windows for both the unit and the program.

a. Run the project once. It produces, sorts, and displays five arrays of 100 integer values each. Now, let's look at the processing involved in more detail.

b. Set stop signs at the following points in *Sorter.p*:

   i. At the second **begin** in **function** *FindMin*.
   ii. At the call to *Swap* in **procedure** *SelectionSort*.
   iii. At the **end** immediately after the call to *Swap* in *SelectionSort*.

Now, open the Observe window and create entries for the following expressions. (By the way, we can't enter an unsubscripted array name in the Observe window, since it refers to a *collection* of values rather than a single one.)

min
i
a[i]
current
where
inArray[current]
inArray[where]
inArray[1]
inArray[2]
inArray[3]

c. Run the project, proceeding from stop sign to stop sign, paying attention to the points listed below. Go through the program slowly until you understand exactly how it works.

   i. As long as you remain in *FindMin*, write down the successive values of *i* and *a[i]* here:

   i :
   a[i] :

   Notice how *FindMin* tracks through the array, finding new minimal values of *a[i]*, until it finds the smallest value at or after position *current*.
   ii. Click on the Text window and verify the locations of the successive minimal elements you noted earlier.

iii. Once you've left *FindMin*, look at the values of *current* (the position of the current array element where the search for the minimal value begins), and *where* (the position of the smallest element after the current position). Watch the *inArray* display to see that *Swap* interchanges the elements in those positions.

iv. Repeat the preceding steps until you have a clear picture of how *SelectionSort* works.

2. Analyzing the Algorithm

As explained in the text, we can describe the efficiency of an algorithm generally as a function of the number of elements the algorithm processes. The Selection Sort algorithm was described as an n^2 algorithm, meaning that in the worst case, sorting a list of n numbers will take no longer than a fixed multiple of n^2 time.

We can get a "ballpark" measure of time by counting the number of instructions performed by an algorithm. This type of measure properly discounts differences among compilers and machines, and focuses on the high-level algorithm. In fact, one of the reasons our PIP performs the sort five times for each run is so that we can gather some data about its efficiency.

a. Let's insert two counters into the Selection Sort algorithm. One will keep track of the number of comparisons needed to perform a particular sort (call it *compareCounter*); the other will count the number of data movements, swaps in this case (call it *swapCounter*). We can modify the program to print these counts out after each sort and to average them over the five sorts of a single run of the program.

  i. Declare *swapCounter* and *compareCounter* as global variables in the main program. Because they will get fairly large, declare both to be of **type** *longint*. This is a nonstandard type that includes integers up to 2,147,483,647.

  ii. Change *FindMin* to a procedure, since it will return more than one value.

  iii. Initialize both variables to zero within the **for** loop in the main program and pass them as parameters to *SelectionSort* and *FindMin*.

  iv. Within *SelectionSort* and *FindMin*, increment these parameters each time a comparison or swap is made.

  v. Finally, remove the array displays and include a *writeln* statement that displays the values of the two counters. The relevant parts of your program should look like this:

```
program Sorter;
  ⋮
  var
    ⋮
    compareCounter, swapCounter : longint;
    ⋮
```

```
      procedure SelectionSort (var inArray: NumArray ; var swaps, comps : longint);
        ⋮
      procedure FindMin (a: NumArray; start: integer;
                         var where: integer ; var swaps, comps : longint);
        ⋮
      begin
        ⋮
        for i : = start + 1 to ARRAYSIZE do
          begin
            comps : = comps + 1;   {Record that we're about to make a comparison.}
            if a[i] < min then
              begin
                ⋮
              end
          end
      end;
      begin   {SelectionSort}
        for current : = 1 to ARRAYSIZE − 1 do
          begin
            FindMin(inArray, current, where, swaps, comps);
            where : = Swap(inArray[current], inArray[where]);
            swaps : = swaps + 1        {Record that we've made a swap.}
          end
      end;   {procedure SelectionSort}
        ⋮
    begin   {Main}
      Setup;
      for trial : = 1 to 5 do
        begin
          swapCounter : = 0;
          compareCounter : = 0;
          BuildArray(theArray);

          SelectionSort(theArray, swapCounter, compareCounter);

          writeln('swaps: ', swapCounter : 1, ' comparisons: ', compareCounter : 1)
        end
    end.   {Main}
```

b. Run the revised project and note the values for swaps and comparisons. Notice that no matter what the original array is, the number of swaps and comparisons is always the same. Why?

c. Since the number of swaps and comparisons depends only on the size of the array, and not its contents, we need look at only one array. Change the **for** loop in the main program by making the upper limit 1, just like the lower limit. Now run your project several times, changing the value of *ARRAYSIZE* in the *Arrays* unit. Record your results below.

ARRAYSIZE	100	200	300	400	500
swaps					
comparisons					

How does the number of swaps depend on the size of the array?

How does the number of comparisons depend on the size of the array? *Hint*: If n is the size of the array, look at $n(n-1)/2$.

Are these numbers consistent with the description of Selection Sort as an n^2 algorithm?

3. Quicksort

If you haven't already done so, now's a good time to review Section 9.5 of the text, where we discuss Hoare's Quicksort algorithm.

a. You'll find the algorithm in the PIP 9 folder. It's in a new main program called *Quicksorter.p*. Remove the *Sorter.p* program from your project and replace it with *Quicksorter.p*.

b. Run the program and verify that it does indeed sort correctly (you may want to set *ARRAYSIZE* back to 100 in the *Arrays* unit).

c. Quicksort, the way we've implemented it, is a recursive algorithm. Recursive algorithms are hard to follow, so let's trace it in action. Put a stop sign at the first recursive call in *Quicksort*, immediately after the line where *Partition* is called. In the Observe window, enter the identifiers *start*, *split*, and *finish*. Run your project and record the first few successive values in the Observe window.

Recall that the heart of Quicksort is to partition a part of the array into two pieces, so that all the elements in the left piece are less than or equal to all the elements in the right piece. The boundaries of the pieces are given by the values *start*, *split*, and *finish*, and these are used as the new boundaries for the recursive calls. For example, if we began with *start* = 1 and *finish* = 100 and *Partition* selected *split* = 81, we would then have two recursive calls with boundaries 1, 81 and 82, 100.

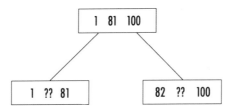

Use the values you recorded to produce a similar tree diagram of some of the calls that *Quicksort* makes.

d. In the text we claim that Quicksort is a faster algorithm than Selection Sort. Let's justify this claim. Using Exercise 2 of this lab as a guide, modify *Quicksorter* so that it counts swaps and comparisons. Run your modified project and record the results.

e. Notice that, unlike the case with Selection Sort, Quicksort performs different numbers of swaps and comparisons on arrays of the same size. To get a better idea of the behavior of Quicksort, modify your program so that it computes the average number of swaps and comparisons over five trials. You'll need two new global variables, to keep running totals of the swaps and comparisons from all five trials.

Once your averaging program is running as it should, try it for various values of *ARRAYSIZE* and record your results below.

ARRAYSIZE	100	200	300	400	500
swaps					
comparisons					

How does the number of swaps depend on the size of the array? If the number of swaps is linear (that is, a multiple of the array size), you should get roughly the same number each time when you divide the number of swaps by the size of the array. Do you?

How does the number of comparisons depend on the size of the array? We can see that the number of comparisons increases faster than linearly, since doubling the size of the array more than doubles the number of comparisons. We might guess that for arrays of size n, Quicksort makes a multiple of $n\log_2 n$ comparisons. If that's so, then you should get roughly the same number each time when you divide the number of comparisons by the $n\log_2 n$. Do you? We'll help you out here: for $n = 100, 200, 300, 400$, and 500, $n\log_2 n$ is approximately 664, 1529, 2469, 3458, and 4483.

Counting swaps and comparisons together, does your evidence indicate that Quicksort is significantly faster than Selection Sort?

Post-Lab Exercises

1. Using the solution to Exercise 19 of Chapter 9 of the text, implement and test Insertion Sort as we did in the lab for Selection Sort. Does it appear that Insertion Sort is an n^2 or $n\log_2 n$ algorithm? How does it rate in efficiency when compared with Selection Sort and Quicksort?

2. Shellsort, named after its inventor, D. L. Shell, looks like this:

```
interval : = ARRAYSIZE div 2;
   repeat
      for i : = 1 to interval do      Use a simple sorting algorithm (like Insertion Sort)
         interval : = interval div 2   to sort the part of the array at locations i, i +
      until interval = 0               interval, i + 2 * interval, i + 3 * interval, . . .
```

For example, if we had *interval* = 4 at some stage, the **for** loop would cause the portion of the array $a[1]$, $a[5]$, $a[9]$, $a[13]$, ... to be sorted first; then the portion $a[2]$, $a[6]$, $a[10]$, $a[14]$, ...; then the portion $a[3]$, $a[7]$, $a[11]$, $a[15]$, ...; and finally the portion $a[4]$, $a[8]$, $a[12]$, $a[16]$, ... After that, the **for** loop would be finished, *interval* would be divided by 2, and the process would continue at the **for** loop again. This is also known as a *diminishing increment sort*. We need not restrict ourselves to intervals that halve each time — a good choice of intervals is ..., 1093, 364, 121, 40, 13, 4, 1. In fact, we can use any sequence of intervals, as long as the last one is 1. The interesting thing is that this algorithm has never been completely analyzed. Implement and test it as we did in the lab. How does it compare with Selection Sort and Quicksort?

3. Implement and test the improvement to Quicksort suggested in Exercise 31 of Chapter 9 of the text.
4. Write a program that simulates a lottery drawing. For example, to simulate the New York State lottery your program would: (1) initialize an array of 54 integers to the numbers 1 to 54, (2) randomly select 6 of the 54 values (disallowing any duplicate numbers), (3) sort the six values chosen (so that they can be displayed in order), and (4) print the sorted list of choices.

10 Heterogeneous Data Structures: Records

L A B O R A T O R Y

Introduction

Records give us the ability to group together different types of information into composite structures that, like arrays, let us access directly both the individual pieces and the structure as a whole. When coupled with arrays, records give us the Pascal tools we need for describing almost any complex data structure. For some problems, like the PIP for this chapter, the difficulty of writing a program lies more in defining an appropriate—that is to say, expressive and useful—data structure than in designing algorithms. Once the central data structures are defined and understood, the program's algorithms tend to come into focus.

Our goals in this lab center on understanding and getting comfortable with the data structures and their uses in a simple word-processing program, named PasWord. It is important that you understand the program so that you can accomplish these exercises. It is essential that by the time you complete the exercises you be comfortable with PasWord, because it is the basis for the lab exercises for the next two chapters, as well as this one.

L A B   O B J E C T I V E S

In this lab, we will:

- Provide you with an opportunity to experience PasWord as a user by experimenting with its commands so that you see how it performs.

- Help you to analyze the behavior of PasWord in detail, paying particular attention to its use of records and other programmer-defined data structures.
- Guide you in completing the program stubs for deleting and changing lines of a document.
- Describe how PasWord can be expanded to perform other useful word-processing operations.

Exercises

1. PasWord in Action

Before looking at PasWord as a programmer would, let's look at it from a user's perspective. Open the PIP 10 folder and add the *DocHandler* unit and the **program** *PasWord* to your generic project. Run the program now. You can use the sample dialog in the text as a model for how to use the program, or just experiment on your own.

Be sure to use all of the available commands (noting, of course, that the Delete and Change commands are, for the moment, unimplemented). Also, try a variety of parameters so that you can witness PasWord's modest error-handling facilities.

2. For the Record

It's now time to review PasWord in greater detail and, as usual, we'll rely on TP's debugging facilities to help us control and analyze the program. If you've had a chance to look at the main program, you'll see that it does little more than get a command character from the operator and then use that character to control a **case** statement that calls one of the document-handling routines. That's simple enough to understand that we'll concentrate for the time being on the *DoInsertion* procedure in the *DocHandler* unit.

  a. Insert stop signs at the following locations in *DoInsertion*:

    i. At the *writeln* call just after the call to *GetALine*.
    ii. At the last **end** in the procedure.

  b. Open the Observe window and create entries for:

    d.totalLines
    d.theLine[1]
    d.theLine[2]
    d.theLine[3]
    d.theLine[4]

Notice we referred to *d*, not *doc*. Why?

  c. Now let's walk through the program.

    i. Enter the command 'i 1' and then the line 'first line'. Step through the procedure using **Step Into** (⌘-I) and keep your eye on the Observe window. When you get to the second stop sign, use the **Go** command (⌘-G, remember) to get out of stepping mode.

How did insertion work? Did the program have to call *ShiftArray?*

ii. Enter the command 'i 2' and then the line 'second line'. Step through the procedure using ⌘-I and keep your eye on the Observe window, as before. When you get to the second stop sign, again use ⌘-G to get out of stepping mode.

How did insertion work? Did the program have to call *ShiftArray* this time?

iii. Enter the command 'i 15' and then the line 'third line'. Follow the same sequence of steps you did before.

How did the program handle the command to insert at the 15th line?

iv. Now we have to proceed carefully. Enter the command 'i 2' and then the line 'new second'. Watch the Observe window very carefully as you step through *ShiftArray*. Make sure you see how *ShiftArray* works. You might want to inspect *i*, *d.theLine[i]*, and *d.theLine[i − 1]* in the Observe window.

In which subprogram was 'new second' actually inserted into the document?

3. Practice

Now that you see how *PasWord* really works, you can begin the process, which will continue through this and the next two labs, of extending PasWord into a fully functional word processor.

a. The first thing to do is to complete the **procedure** *DoDeletion*. The *stub* that is currently in *DocHandler* has correctly defined and placed the procedure heading. It's up to you to fill in the body. As usual, it helps to think about the problem in English before plunging ahead and trying to write your algorithm in Pascal.

Deleting a given line from a document seems slightly more straightforward than inserting one. Given our representation of a document, it's not as if anything actually gets "thrown away." It's more a matter of moving each of the lines after the deleted one down one spot in the document, thereby deleting the desired line. There are two times when this approach won't work, and both correspond to *boundary* cases. One is when we want to delete the last line of a document. In this case, if we simply decrement the counter for the number of lines in the document by 1, the program will act as if the last line had been deleted — just as we hoped.

The second boundary case is when there are no lines yet in the document, in which case none can be deleted. Probably, the thing to do here would be just to print out a message and leave the empty document alone.

The best place to start in implementing this approach in Pascal is to look at the **procedure** *DoInsertion*. It presents nearly an "inverse" algorithm to deletion and should serve as a model for your *DoDeletion* procedure. Write it and test it now.

b. Now, how can you accomplish the changing of a particular line, as prescribed by **procedure** *DoChange*? In human terms, we tend to think of changing a line of a document with an eraser; that is, we alter the line rather than replace the entire thing. Another model of change is one of literally replacing one line of a document with another (perhaps using two procedures that are already implemented?). Which approach is better here? The first is probably more efficient, but the second builds directly on what you have already written. Complete *DoChange* now, using either of these approaches, and test it out with a variety of parameters.

While you're designing and implementing *DoChange*, be sure to give some thought to ease of use. For example, it would probably be a good idea to display the line the operator has chosen to change.

Post-Lab Exercises

1. Modify *DoInsertion* so that it automatically performs multiple insertions. That is, the command 'i 8' would now be interpreted to insert new text beginning at line 8 for as many lines as the user types. New lines would be added in successive positions to the document until an empty line (length = 0) was entered. You could either modify the existing *DoInsertion* procedure or write another multiple insertion version that uses the original.

2. Modify *DoDeletion* so that it takes two parameters, in the same way that the *ShowDoc* procedure does. The aim here is that the command 'd 2 6 ' will delete lines 2 through 6 in the document, if they exist, and take appropriate action if they don't (as does *ShowDoc*).

3. Implement a Find command that searches the document from the beginning until it finds the first occurrence of a given substring. If it finds the substring in question, it should display the line in which it was found. If the string is not found, a message indicating this fact should be displayed. You might want to look back at the string subprogram *Pos* in Chapter 6.

CHAPTER

11 External Data Structures: Files

L A B O R A T O R Y

Introduction

As complex and interesting as our word processor from Chapter 10 was, it wasn't particularly useful. While it automated the processes of creating and editing documents, it failed to implement perhaps the most significant feature of a word processor—the ability to save a document and recall it for future editing. This general ability to save information to and read information from files is essential to virtually every application program—from word processors to spreadsheets to databases to Pascal compilers. Without this feature, you would have to type in every chapter's PIP for yourself and then reenter it each time you started the TP system.

The PIP for this chapter, named PasWord 2.0, is an extended version of PasWord from Chapter 10. PasWord 2.0 allows you to save and recall documents as textfiles, using techniques much like those your programs have always used for reading from the keyboard and writing information to the screen. In this lab, we will investigate the file-handling capabilities of the PIP and show how they can be upgraded even further to allow more features to be added.

L AB OBJECTIVES

In this lab, we will:

- Encourage you to experiment with PasWord 2.0's file-handling operations, *SaveDoc* and *ReadDoc.*
- Describe the TP-specific file-handling commands that are used in the PIP.

External Data Structures: Files

L A B O R A T O R Y

Introduction

As complex and interesting as our word processor from Chapter 10 was, it wasn't particularly useful. While it automated the processes of creating and editing documents, it failed to implement perhaps the most significant feature of a word processor—the ability to save a document and recall it for future editing. This general ability to save information to and read information from files is essential to virtually every application program—from word processors to spreadsheets to databases to Pascal compilers. Without this feature, you would have to type in every chapter's PIP for yourself and then reenter it each time you started the TP system.

The PIP for this chapter, named PasWord 2.0, is an extended version of PasWord from Chapter 10. PasWord 2.0 allows you to save and recall documents as textfiles, using techniques much like those your programs have always used for reading from the keyboard and writing information to the screen. In this lab, we will investigate the file-handling capabilities of the PIP and show how they can be upgraded even further to allow more features to be added.

L AB OBJECTIVES

In this lab, we will:

- Encourage you to experiment with PasWord 2.0's file-handling operations, *SaveDoc* and *ReadDoc.*
- Describe the TP-specific file-handling commands that are used in the PIP.

- Use TP's file-handling commands to add a Save As... operation to PasWord 2.0.
- Guide you through upgrading PasWord to version 2.2, as described in the text.
- Help you to implement menu commands for explicitly opening and closing files in PasWord.
- Show you how internal files can be used to implement Cut, Copy, and Paste commands.

Exercises

1. Running PasWord 2.0

PasWord 2.0 should seem quite familiar to you, in that you have used version 1.0 extensively and even contributed some code to the new version. In terms of its basic document-handling operations, PasWord 2.0 is in fact nearly identical to the original. Where it differs from version 1.0 is in its file-handling features, and those aren't altogether obvious from just looking at the code.

a. Run *PasWord2* now. Notice that when the program starts you are asked to either start a new document or open an existing one. The first time, answer 'n' for a new document. You can now go about inserting, deleting, changing, and printing lines exactly as you did in PasWord 1.0. Do so now, creating a document with five to ten lines of text.

b. Now, choose 'q' to invoke the Quit operation. You will be asked if you want to save the current document before quitting. Enter 's' to save it. When asked to provide a file name, enter 'mydoc'.

c. After the project stops running, select **Quit** from the **File** menu and look at your Macintosh desktop. There should be a file named *mydoc*. Restart TP now and open your project again. Run the project and, when asked to open an existing file, enter 'O' for open. When prompted for the name of a file to open, enter 'mydoc', followed by a Return. If you then enter command 'p 1 10' to print lines 1 through 10 of the current document, your document as saved should appear on the screen.

2. PasWord 2.0: TP Version

We mentioned that the version of the PIP in the text was a standard Pascal implementation of PasWord. If you look closely at the TP version of the program on your disk, you'll notice a few minor differences between it and the standard. These differences relate to PasWord's handling of files, particularly to the opening of files.

This shouldn't surprise you, since files are the feature of Pascal that vary most from system to system. Why? Because files are by and large external to Pascal programs and, thus, tend to be stored and accessed in ways that depend more on the computer/operating system they are implemented on than on the version of Pascal from which they are accessed.

a. In both the text and disk version of PasWord 2.0, all access to files is done through a file variable, *docFile*, declared to be of **type** *text*. Remember, *text* is shorthand for **file of** *char*, and textfiles are the type of file you are already used to dealing with. The standard Pascal input file is a textfile that is associated automatically with the keyboard. The screen is referred to from programs as the standard Pascal text output file. How, though, do we associate other nonstandard file variables in our programs with honest-to-goodness files on our Macintosh desktop?

These links are created in TP by modified forms of the statements that open files. TP's *reset* and *rewrite* statements do more than just open files and specify whether they are to be open in read- or write-only mode. They also serve to make a logical connection between a file variable and a real file name. Just as an integer variable can take on a variety of integer values during the course of execution of a program, so too can file variables be associated with different file names. This way PasWord 2.0, for example, is not constrained to read and write the exact same file every time it runs.

Look at **procedure** *SaveDoc* in the disk version of *DocHandler2.u*. Notice, first, that there is a string variable named *fileName* declared locally. Notice, too, that *fileName* receives its value from a *readln* statement, which reads a string from the keyboard (after prompting the user to enter the name of a file). The *rewrite* statement that follows, *rewrite(f, fileName)*, acts like an assignment statement for the file variable *f*. It temporarily links *f* with an external file that has as its name the value of *fileName*—that is, whatever the user typed in. That link remains (or, you could say that *f* has that value) until either *f* is closed, rewritten, or reset, or the program ends.

The same type of exchange takes place in **procedure** *ReadDoc*. The user is prompted for a file name, the value is stored in a string variable *fileName* (any string variable will do), and that name is linked with a file variable. In this case, the link is made via a *reset* statement, which opens the specified file in read-only mode. Note that the second parameter of both *reset* and *rewrite* can be a string literal, in addition to a string variable. Remember, too, that once a file variable has been reset or rewritten subsequent references to files in *read*, *write*, or *close* statements are all made in terms of file variables, not file names.

b. The method outlined above for soliciting file names in string form from a user is not particularly Mac-like. In fact, if you type in a file name that does not exist and try to *reset* it, a run-time error is produced. It turns out that TP provides two built-in functions that help us to solicit file names from a user according to more standard Mac protocol.

The **function** *NewFileName* displays a Macintosh dialog box like the kind you see when you go to save a program file in TP. The function allows the user to specify a file name and to change directories or disks; and it returns as its value a string holding the specified file name (along with Mac-specific designations describing where it resides). If the user clicks the **Cancel** button, the function returns the empty string, which we indicate as '' (two adjacent single quotes). A sample call to *NewFileName* would look like:

```
var
  f : text;
  fileName : string;
  ⋮
  fileName : = NewFileName('Save the file as: ');
  if fileName <> " then    {The user does want to create a file.}
    begin
      rewrite(f, fileName);
      ⋮
    end
```

The string parameter to *NewFileName* is displayed in the dialog box, and whatever name has been entered when the OK box is clicked is the value returned by the function and assigned to, in this case, variable *fileName*. *FileName* can then be used directly, as in *rewrite(f, fileName)*, to open a file in write-only mode.

An analogous function for opening existing files, named *OldFileName*, presents an Open File dialog box from which you use the mouse to select a file from any disk and folder. If the user clicks the **Cancel** button, the function returns the empty string. A sample call to *OldFileName* is

```
var
  f : text;
  fileName : string;
  ⋮
  fileName : = OldFileName('Open file named: ');
  if fileName <> " then    {The user does want to open a file.}
    begin
      reset(f, fileName);
      ⋮
    end
```

Modify your version of *DocHandler2.u* to make use of **function** *NewFileName* (in *SaveDoc*) and *OldFileName* (in *ReadDoc*), instead of using prompts and *read*s from the keyboard.

Rerun the project to see how the Mac-specific routines facilitate the naming and opening of files.

3. An *Open* and *Close* Case

Now that our program has the ability to read and write documents to disk files, why not give the user some control over when files get read and written? In the current version of PasWord, the user gets a single opportunity to open a file — when the program starts — and a single chance to save one — after quitting. A more realistic and flexible scenario is to include Open and Close as commands available to the user from the main menu.

a. The good news is that we already have procedures written, *SaveDoc* and *ReadDoc*, that carry out these operations. Making them available at any time to the user is merely a matter of changing the main menu to allow the user to choose these operations directly and at any time.

The only trick to beware of is that, unless we redesign the program significantly (which we'll defer until the next lab), there can only be one *current* document at a given time. This means that we must avoid two possible sources of confusion in the program. In the first case, we must take care not to allow a file to be opened when there is already a document in memory. (We could give the user the opportunity to close and save the current document before opening another.) In the second, we should not attempt to close a file if the current document is empty.

How can you tell whether there is a current document? How would you use this test to make the Open and Close commands robust?

b. Extend your version of PasWord 2.0 to include menu commands for opening and closing a document. Don't forget to include the new Open and Close commands in the *GetCommand* procedure. Macintosh applications use agreed-upon standard command characters for these operations, as you can see by looking at TP's File menu. The standard character for Open is 'O' and, for some reason, the command character for Close is 'W'.

4. Upgrading to PasWord 2.2

In the interest of providing examples of file-processing techniques, the text guides you gradually through three file-processing versions of PasWord, labelled 2.0, 2.1, and 2.2. We can—and we're going to—jump directly from 2.0 to 2.2 without missing a beat in terms of programming. Review, now, Section 11.5 of your text, wherein we describe general files.

At the end of that section, we show how your program can be upgraded to version 2.2 by defining a *docFile* as a **file of** *Document*, as opposed to a textfile. Make the changes described in Section 11.4 to upgrade your program to version 2.2, now, and test them out.

5. The New and Improved PasWord 2.2

In recent years the terms *copy*, *cut*, and *paste* have been borrowed from the world of graphic design and applied to word processing. They describe the process of removing or duplicating text from one part of a document and placing it (pasting it) into another. In commercial-grade word processors, such operations can be applied to arbitrary selections of text—that is, to any collection of characters, from a subset of a line to characters spanning many lines.

While we cannot yet get quite that sophisticated, we know everything we need to implement these operations on a line-by-line basis. For example, we can imagine in our current PasWord framework providing menu operations as follows:

Cut line1 line2, which removes lines numbered *line1* through (and including) *line2* from the current document and saves them somewhere until another Cut or Copy command is invoked.

Copy line1 line2, which copies, but does not remove, lines numbered *line1* through (and including) *line2* from the current document and saves them somewhere until another Cut or Copy command is invoked.

Paste line1, which places a copy of whatever was most recently cut or copied into the current document, beginning at line *line1*.

There are a number of familiar terms in these descriptions. It seems, for example, that we have subprograms around that will be helpful in removing and inserting lines at successive locations in a document. The one term in these descriptions that has no immediate analog in our PasWord is *somewhere*. What and where is this place that temporarily stores text for later use? In the vernacular, this place is commonly referred to as the *Clipboard*. Do you have any ideas for how a clipboard might be implemented? Think about it.

How about using a temporary file? These are discussed in the text in Section 11.5, where we describe a procedure, *DeleteFirst*, for deleting the first element of a file.

Answer the following questions about a temporary clipboard file:

How should the file variable *clipFile* be declared — that is, what is its type?

Where — in what part of the program — should it be declared?

How should it be opened — in read-only or write-only mode?

When does its mode change?

What combination of statements would change its mode?

When should we write to the temporary file?

When should we read from the temporary file?

Use your answers to help you to implement a clipboard as a temporary file. Then, use the Clipboard to implement *Cut*, *Copy*, and *Paste* procedures as described. Finally, change the main menu to allow the user to invoke these commands directly. Name the resulting program PasWord 2.3. Again, don't forget to change *GetCommand*. You can look at TP's Edit menu for the standard command characters for these operations: 'X' for Cut, 'C' for Copy, and 'V' for Paste. To help you out, you can declare a file anonymously in TP: to open a **file** *clipFile*, for example, you can issue the command *reset(clipFile)* or *rewrite(clipFile)*, with no file name. In TP, you are not allowed to close an anonymous file, so leave the *close* command out. The temporary file will vanish when you quit the program.

Rehash

- Files are opened by using the built-in **procedure**s *reset* (for reading from a file) and *rewrite* (for writing information onto a file). In TP, both procedures require a file variable and a file name as parameters. For example, to prepare a file named *My File* for reading, we might make the procedure call *reset(f,* 'My File')*, which would establish a logical link in the program from the file variable *f* and the file named *My File*. Thereafter, any reference to *f* would be understood to be a reference to *My File* on the disk.
- The only time we can dispense with the file name is when we create a temporary file that will not be saved on disk. In TP, we may not *close* a temporary file.
- The TP **procedure** *close(fileVariable)* is used when you are finished reading or writing from a file. This severs any logical link between the file variable and a physical file on a disk. Any named file that has been opened by *reset* or *rewrite* should be closed before the program ends.
- The Mac-specific **function** *NewFileName* displays a standard dialog box allowing the operator to choose a name for a file along with the location where the file will be saved. *NewFileName* returns a string equal to the name the user chose for the file. If the user clicks the **Cancel** button in the dialog box, the function returns the empty string (so the program can check

whether the user decided to save the file or not). *NewFileName* is commonly used like this:

```
var
  f : text;
  fileName : string;
    ⋮
  fileName : = NewFileName('Save the file as: ');
  if fileName <> " then    {The user does want to create a file.}
    begin
      rewrite(f, fileName);
        ⋮
    end
```

- The Mac-specific **function** *OldFileName* displays another standard dialog box, allowing the operator to select an existing file to be opened. *OldFileName* returns a string equal to the name of the file the user selected. If the user clicks the **Cancel** button in the dialog box, the function returns the empty string (so the program can check whether the user decided to open a file or not). *OldFileName* is commonly used like this:

```
var
  f : text;
  fileName : string;
    ⋮
  fileName : = OldFileName('Open the file named: ');
  if fileName <> " then    {The user does want to open a file.}
    begin
      reset(f, fileName);
        ⋮
    end
```

The string prompt in *OldFileName* is needed, but—unlike the prompt in *NewFileName*—it never appears in the dialog box. In the words of the Macintosh programming bible, *Inside Macintosh*, vol. 1 (Reading, MA: Addison-Wesley, 1985), "The prompt parameter is ignored; it's there for historical purposes only." The ways of the programming wizard are often inscrutable.

Post-Lab Exercises

1. Write a program, *Converter*, which reads documents produced using PasWord 2.0 (textfiles) and converts them into binary files that are suitable as input for PasWord version 2.2. You have seen all of the commands—and even some of the exact procedures—that will help you write *Converter*.
2. Rewrite PasWord version 2.2 using primitive input/output operations (*get* and *put*) only.

12 Variables on the Fly: Pointers

L A B O R A T O R Y

Introduction

At this point in its evolution there are only two significant drawbacks that keep PasWord from being a realistic and functional word processor. The first is the lack of a more contemporary user interface. We mentioned right from the start that to develop a window-based, screen-oriented application requires an attention to machine-dependent detail that is inconsistent with the more immediate goals of our text/lab package.

The second drawback is fair game for this text — and this lab. It has to do with the limited size of a PasWord document. Up to now, a constant (*MAXLINES*) was used to constrain documents to 64 lines. Granted, the value of the constant could be changed to 100, or 1000, or 10,000, but this would, particularly for small documents, waste vast amounts of memory and still limit larger documents.

The solution to handling data structures whose sizes may vary widely, even while a program is being used, is to implement them dynamically by using pointers. This lab, then, presents a pointer-based implementation of PasWord, which overcomes these size constraints (or, at least, manages the size of a document more efficiently than any of the previous versions).

L A B   O B J E C T I V E S

In this lab, we will:

- Demonstrate and give you experience using PasWord 3.0, the pointer-based implementation of PasWord that is this chapter's PIP.

- Guide you in analyzing the PIP in detail, particularly noting the use of pointers and linked lists.

- Help you to complete the program by implementing the remaining subprogram stubs for modifying documents.

- Describe how and encourage you to extend PasWord 3.0 to include some of the operations we had included in earlier versions (such as Find and multiple insertions).

Exercises

1. Appearances Are Deceiving: Running PasWord 3.0

You'll notice that the PIP 12 folder contains only the **unit** *DocHandler3.u*, and no program. That's because all of the changes in PasWord 3.0 occur in the unit and not in the main program. To build the project for this lab, all you have to do is include *DocHandler3* and the PasWord main program from Lab 11 (don't forget to change the **uses** directive in the main program). Run your project now and try it out. When asked whether to open an existing document or start a new one, enter 'n' for New (documents created by PasWord 2.1, 2.2, and 2.3 are incompatible with PasWord 3.0). Create a new document, edit it (note that the Delete and Change operations are, again, unimplemented), and save it. Restart the program and this time open the file you just created. Do some more editing and quit.

2. Inside the Program

From the perspective of a user, PasWord 3.0 should look to you just like previous implementations of the program. Looking at the program code, however, immediately reveals significant differences from past versions.

a. Instead of telling you how to analyze in detail the behavior of PasWord 3.0, we'll give you some latitude. You can determine for yourself where to set stop signs and what entries to make in the Observe window. Answering the following questions may provide you with some direction. Assume that you will start the project by creating a new document and will follow the basic sequence of operations described in Exercise 1.

    i. In what approximate order (depending on how many lines you insert into the new document) will the main program and the subprograms get invoked?

ii. Identify one or two statements in each portion of the program where something significant happens in terms of PasWord 3.0's use of pointers.

iii. In each of the preceding statements mentioned, which quantities (variables, parameters, expressions) get inspected or manipulated by the statement?

b. Go ahead, now. Set your stop signs and make the entries in the Observe window that will reveal to you the inner workings of PasWord 3.0. Run the program, stopping as dictated by your stop signs and stepping through those parts of the program that make extensive use of pointers and linked lists.
   Two notes of caution and advice:

i. While it is perfectly legal to do so, looking in the Observe window at the value of a pointer variable is usually not too informative. Remember, the value of a pointer variable is an address in memory — typically a very long number represented in hexadecimal (base 16) notation. Most often, what you are interested in when analyzing a program are the values of things that pointers point at. So, to see the real data that p points to, your entry in the Observe window should be $p\hat{}.theLine$.

ii. Your goal in this exercise is to come to grips with PasWord 3.0. Doing so requires that you have the ability to read and interpret an existing program. These analytical skills are essential to becoming a good programmer. They serve you in debugging, extending, modifying, and maintaining both your and other people's programs. We have done our best throughout these lab sessions to help you to develop and appreciate what is involved in analyzing a program. Now, it's up to you.

3. Filling in the Holes: *DoDeletion* and *DoChange*

As we have done in other implementations of PasWord, we have left certain of the subprograms in stub form for you to fill in. Doing so allows us to develop a program incrementally, adding functionality as we go along, without disturbing a working program. It's time, almost, to fill in the code for **procedures** *DoDeletion* and *DoChange*. Before doing so, it might be helpful to look back at the previous implementations of these two procedures to refresh your memory. The fact that the new versions must be implemented using pointers and linked lists doesn't change the fact that they must address and solve the same problems that the old ones did.

a. Before attempting to write *DoDeletion* remember, first, that because we're using pointers here, there is no need for "moving" lines of a document around. What we'll do instead is rearrange the values of pointers to "point around" the unwanted line. Second, think about what to do in the boundary cases, when you want to delete the first or last line in a document. Notice, too, that we have been thoughtful enough to include subprograms for deleting the head of a list, for deleting an arbitrary cell from a list, and for finding an arbitrary cell in a list. If you can describe your deletion algorithm in those terms, you'll be in business.

Write and test your pointer-based version of *DoDeletion* now.

b. Implement *DoChange* now. **Function** *FindNth* should serve you well here. Test *DoChange* with a variety of parameters before proceeding.

4. Beyond PasWord 3.0

There are a couple of obvious extensions to PasWord that we have mentioned in previous labs that we are now in a position to implement in PasWord 3.0. Using our current pointer-based implementation, coupled with TP's string-handling capabilities, should allow us to develop subprograms for finding occurrences of particular words in a document and for inserting multiple lines into a document all at once.

a. Finding the first occurrence of a word in a document doesn't sound too intimidating, even in PasWord 3.0. We traverse the document line by line, checking each to see if it contains the word in question. If the word is found, the line in which it was found is displayed. If it isn't found, a message indicating so is printed.

You can use the *SaveDoc* procedure as a model for traversing through a document line by line. The nonstandard predefined **function** *Pos* can be helpful here. *Pos(substr, str)* returns an integer indicating the position of the first occurrence of *substr* in *str* and returns zero if *substr* doesn't occur in *str*.

Try writing a Find command by implementing a *Find* procedure as described here and changing the main menu to allow the user to invoke the command directly.

b. We noted in an earlier lab the awkwardness of inserting lines into PasWord documents. This is due to the "one line at a time" nature of the Insert command. We would like, as we did before, to modify the Insert command so that each time it is invoked it accepts as many lines of text as the user wants to enter (each line ending with a return). Users will signal that they are done inserting lines by typing an empty line (that is, typing just Return). The new Insert command should look the same to the user as the original, in the sense that it is still invoked with a single parameter indicating the line at which the insertions are to begin.

Revise your *Insert* operation to allow multiple insertions now, and test it out.

Post-Lab Exercises

1. Use the Find command to define a *Find Next* command. Like a Find command, Find Next searches a body of text for a given word. Unlike Find, Find Next begins its search from wherever it left off—not always from the start of a document. That is, when first invoked it finds the first occurrence of the word in question. The next time it is invoked, it finds the second, and then the third, and so on.

2. Once your Find Next command works, you should be able to implement a global search-and-replace command. That is, a Replace command should take two string parameters and replace every occurrence of the first string with the second string, throughout the document.

Introduction to Abstract
Data Types: Linked Lists

13

L A B O R A T O R Y

Introduction

Given the unusual nature of the PIPs for this chapter (they're not programs at all, but TP units), it seems fitting that the format of this lab differs from that of all previous labs. As opposed to concentrating on reading, running, analyzing, and extending a program, we will concentrate, as does the text, on defining an abstract data type (ADT, for short). Our goal is to describe a collection of data and subprogram declarations of general utility and to encapsulate them as a TP unit. Then, any program that wants to use these declarations can do so by including a **uses** clause that refers to our ADT.

Our primary consideration, then, is which ADT to implement. The text already provides a description of two different implementations of a LIST ADT, each of which defines both the data structures and the most common list-manipulation operations. It would be nice if, as has been the case in all other labs, these PIPs (or, more accurately, UIPs, for "Units in Progress") were somehow useful to our chosen ADT. It would also be nice, we thought, if the chosen ADT were of demonstrated utility to a variety of Pascal programs and was not already implemented as part of the Pascal standard.

Any ideas? What about defining a STRING Abstract Data Type? The fact that strings are implemented and included in TP as an extension to standard Pascal is testimony to their general utility. In fact, almost all of our PIPs since Chapter 6 make use of strings.

Strings also have the virtue that they can be described as lists of characters. Think about it for a minute. . . . What do we do with strings? In TP we can access a string's individual elements, we can determine a string's length, we can search for substrings in a string, we can insert and delete substrings from strings, we can determine if a string is empty, or we can try to access a "badPosition" in a string, that is, a nonexistent position. We make the point in the text that lists can be thought of as the starting point for a discussion of ADTs, and in this lab you'll see why.

L A B　　O B J E C T I V E S

In this lab, we will:

- Help you to appreciate the virtues of abstract data types as implemented by TP units.
- Guide you in using an existing ADT to define a (not so) new one of your own.
- Demonstrate how different implementations of ADTs do not (and should not) affect the programs that use them.

Exercises

1. Strings as Lists: The Basics

In describing a string (or any) ADT we must first decide how the central data structure is to be represented. Typically, this decision is made with an eye toward implementing the operations that will be included with the data structure in the ADT, and with the expected tradeoffs between efficiency of storage and efficiency of use. In this particular case, we are further constrained by our desire to make use of the list ADTs that compose our PIPs.

There are, to be sure, other (and in some ways better) approaches to describing a string, but we will define it to be simply a list of elements of **type** *char*. This can be accomplished directly by revising one of our list units so that its *DataType* is *char*.

a. Open **unit** *ArrayList.u* from the PIP 13 folder on your Pascal's Triangle disk. Use the **Save As...** command from the **File** menu to save a copy and name it *ArrayListChar.u*.

Now, edit the new unit so that its first **type** declaration reads:

DataType = char;

b. Use the **New** command from the **File** menu to open a new Program window, which you'll use to create a string ADT. Enter the following into the Text window:

unit ArrayString;
{An array-based implementation of strings.　}
{Uses the array-based list ADT from Chapter 13.}
interface
　uses
　　ArrayListChar;

```
type
    OurString = {to be filled in};

function ElementOfString(s: OurString; i: integer): char;
function LengthOfString(s: OurString): integer;
procedure ReadlnString(var s: OurString);
procedure WritelnString(s: OurString);

implementation
    function ElementOfString {(s: OurString; i: integer): char} ;
    {for selecting elements}
    begin
        {to be filled in}
    end;

    function LengthOfString {(s: OurString): integer} ;
    {returns the current length}
    begin
        {to be filled in}
    end;

    procedure ReadlnString {(var s: OurString)} ;
    {for reading strings from standard input only}
    begin
        {to be filled in}
    end;

    procedure WritelnString {(s: OurString)} ;
    {for writing strings to standard output only}
    begin
        {to be filled in}
    end;
end. {of unit ArrayString}
```

First, save this new file as *ArrayString.u*. Now, to fill in the details.

c. The first and most obvious omission is the declaration of **type** *OurString*. As with all of the other declarations in this unit, we want to exploit the fact that we have a complete list ADT available to use. So, how do we define *OurString*? Having revised our version of the list unit to define lists of *char*s, we can simply describe *OurString* as being of **type** *List*.

    Make this change now and save **unit** *ArrayString*.

d. Now we can begin to implement the basic operations we would expect to have available to apply to elements of **type** *OurString*. We've included these operations based on their demonstrated utility throughout our PIPs. We have outlined them for you in the unit as:

function *ElementOfString(s, i)*: Given our choice to refer to a string as a list of characters (as opposed, say, to an **array of** *char*), we must define our own selector operation. *ElementOfString* returns the *i*-th character of

OurString s, if one exists; else, it displays an error message and returns the null character, *chr(0)*.

function *LengthOfString(s)*: Returns a non-negative integer representing the current length of its parameter.

procedure *ReadlnString(s)*: Reads a line of characters from the keyboard up to but not including the end-of-line mark, stores it in parameter *s*, and discards the mark from the input buffer.

procedure *WritelnString(s)*: Displays the value of *s* on the standard output device, followed by a return.

You should be ready to fill in the implementations of each of these subprograms. Look in **unit** *ArrayListChar* for subprograms that can help with the two functions. The list unit, along with the descriptions of character I/O we provided in Chapter 6, should give you all you need to implement the two procedures.

We'll get you started (barely) by showing an implementation of **function** *LengthOfString*:

```
function LengthOfString {(s : OurString;)} ;
begin
   LengthOfString : = LLength(s)
end;
```

Fill in the remaining implementations, save, and compile your new unit.

2. Unit Testing

The good thing about units is that, once properly defined, they can be used by any program. The bad news is that you need a program to test them. We can't run your string unit without including it (and **unit** *ArrayListChar*) in a new project that contains a main program that uses it.

a. Create a new program file as follows (or, you can take one of your earlier programs that uses strings and revise it to use the **type** *OurString* instead).

```
program StringTest1;
   uses
      ArrayListChar;
      ArrayString;
   var
      s : OurString;
      i : integer;
   begin
      writeln('Please enter a string at the prompt, followed by Return.');
      writeln('Just a Return terminates processing.');
      write('>');
      ReadlnString(s);
      while LengthOfString(s) > 0 do
```

```
begin
    writeln('The string entered was:');
    writelnString(s);
    writeln;
    writeln('The first character of the string entered was:', ElementOfString(s, 1));
    writeln;
    writeln('The last character of the string entered was:', ElementOfString(s,LengthOfString(s)));
    writeln;
    writeln('Please enter a string at the prompt, followed by Return.');
    writeln('Just a Return terminates processing.');
    write('>');
    ReadlnString(s)
end
end.
```

b. Build a new project, named *ArrayStringTest.π* (you can use the generic project, if you wish), which includes — in this order — the standard runtime and interface libraries, **unit** *ArrayListChar*, **unit** *ArrayString*, and **program** *StringTest1.p*. Check the project to make sure everything compiles and fits together properly.

c. Run the new project to test out your new string ADT.

3. Any List Will Do

We've mentioned that the virtue of units, and ADTs in general, is that they effectively hide the details of implementation from programs that use them. In fact, we can run the same program for testing our string ADT using a completely different implementation of strings, and — if all goes well — it shouldn't make any difference to the **program** *StringTest1*. Let's reimplement strings using our pointer-based list unit.

a. To implement strings using **unit** *LinkedList.u* we must retrace a few — but not all — of our steps from Exercise 2.

    i. Open **unit** *LinkedList* and save it as *LinkedListChar*. Edit the new copy to use *char* as its basic *DataType*.

    ii. Save **unit** *ArrayString.u* as *LinkedString.u* (this doesn't destroy the original).

    iii. Edit **unit** *LinkedString* so that it **uses** *LinkedListChar*, as opposed to *ArrayListChar*.

    iv. Save **program** *StringTest1* as *StringTest2* and edit *StringTest2* so that it **uses** *LinkedListChar* and *LinkedString*.

    v. Build a new project named LinkedStringTest.π that includes, in addition to the standard libraries, **unit** *LinkedListChar*, **unit** *LinkedString*, and **program** *StringTest2*.

b. Now, run the project LinkedStringTest, and it should appear exactly the same as did the array implementation.

Post-Lab Exercises

1. Extend both of your preceding string ADTs to include the equivalent of TP's string operations for data of **type** *OurString*. That is, implement:

   function *PosString(substr, str: OurString): integer;*
   function *ConcatString(s1, s2: OurString): OurString;*
   function *CopyString(source: OurString; index, count: integer): OurString;*
   procedure *InsertString(source: OurString;* **var** *dest: OurString; index: integer);*
   procedure *DeleteString(***var** *dest: OurString; index, count: integer);*

   Don't forget that you've got your list units to work with in implementing these operations.

2. Extend your string ADT to include procedures that allow *OurString*s to be written to and read from textfiles other than the standard input and output files.

3. Revise your final version of PasWord to use the list units described in this chapter.